THE
HELL
THERE IS

THE
HELL
THERE IS

An Exploration of an Often-Rejected
Doctrine of the Church

MSGR. CHARLES POPE

TAN Books
Gastonia, North Carolina

Cover design by Jordan Avery
Cover image: *The Last Judgement, Illustration from the Dore Bible, 1816.* Engraving by Gustave Dore. Universal History Archive/UIG / Bridgeman Images.

ISBN: 978-1-5051-3364-6
Kindle ISBN: 978-1-5051-3501-5
ePUB ISBN: 978-1-5051-3500-8

Published in the United States by
TAN Books
PO Box 269
Gastonia, NC 28053
www.TANBooks.com
Printed in the United States of America

Enter by the narrow gate;
for the gate is wide and the way is easy,
that leads to destruction,
and those who enter by it are many.
For the gate is narrow, and the way is hard,
that leads to life, and those who find it are few.

—Matthew 7:13–14

Contents

Preface

Of all the theological errors commonly held today, the most popular is surely the denial of the doctrine of hell. Even among the more devout, such as those who go to daily Mass, the teaching that God would send or consign anyone to hell is routinely dismissed. If it exists at all, for many, it is largely empty, except perhaps for a few serial killers or genocidal maniacs like Hitler. But for the vast majority—Catholic, non-Catholic, and atheist—hell is a very remote possibility. Never mind that Jesus taught just the opposite, say that "few" are on the narrow road of Salvation and that "many" prefer the darkness (Jn 3:19) and are on the wide road that leads to hell (see Mt 7:13; Lk 13:24). Never mind that twenty-one of Jesus's thirty-eight parables feature scenes of judgment where some are saved and others are lost. There are sheep and goats, wheat and tares, those on the right, those on the left, wise virgins and foolish virgins, and so forth. Indeed, most of the teachings on hell come right from the mouth of Jesus. But for most people, none of this matters.

Some years ago, I was preaching on heaven and hell since the Gospel for that Sunday was of the wide and narrow roads just mentioned. Afterward, a woman approached me, angry that I had mentioned hell at all, and said, "Father, I didn't hear the Jesus I know in your words today." I replied,

"But Ma'am, I was quoting Him directly." She didn't miss a beat and simply replied, "Well, we know He never really said that." Her rejection of hell signals a deeper problem: her rejection of the Scriptures as the inspired and inerrant word of God. The Second Vatican Council affirmed clearly: "Holy Mother Church has firmly and with absolute constancy held, and continues to hold, that the four Gospels just named, whose historical character the Church unhesitatingly asserts, faithfully hand on what Jesus Christ, while living among men, really did and taught for their eternal salvation until the day He was taken up into heaven" (*Dei Verbum* 19).

So she, and none of us, are free to declare that what the Gospels clearly and repeatedly tell us Jesus actually said, He did not actually say. We must affirm the historicity and accuracy of these accounts as the Church requires (see also *CCC* 126).

Her retort also signals another part of the problem: that the "Jesus I know," the "god of my understanding" just wouldn't warn of hell or permit souls to end up there. In our time, God has largely been refashioned and trivialized. The Father has become a doting grandfather, and Jesus has become a harmless hippie. Gone is the God of Scripture, and He is replaced by the "Jesus I know," and the "god of my understanding" who just wouldn't do such a thing. In the past, imagining your own God and worshiping it was called idolatry. Today, most people think they have a perfect right to imagine a god of their own, the "god within" who almost always happens to agree with them. This refashioned "god" is a benign sort of fellow or power who isn't too worked up about the things said by the God of Scripture or the God described by the Church. Hence, at best, God is trivialized and His revealed word is set aside. At worst, God is wholly replaced by another self-fabricated god.

In addition, we have underestimated the seriousness of sin and what it does to harden our hearts against the True God, His kingdom, and its realities and virtues. Sin also darkens our minds, making it difficult to endure the glorious bright light of truth. We fail to comprehend that only those rendered perfect can enter into His holiness or endure His presence. It just doesn't occur to us that our sins render us unfit and incapable of withstanding the awesome and bright glory of God and the temperature of His love.

And hence today, with the widespread trivialization of the divine and a diminished sense of sin, the true God and His teachings revealed in Scripture seem too hard and harsh for the "loving and merciful" god of my understanding. Is God love? Yes! Is He merciful? Yes! But too often today, love is reduced to mere kindness, and mercy is preached without the repentance that opens its floodgates. Hence, appeals to God's love and mercy are not meant in the biblical sense where mercy presupposes sin and our acknowledgment of it as such, and love is not some cheap grace that only affirms but a strong godly love which seeks as its goal that we be "perfect as your heavenly Father is perfect."

The work to render us perfect and to attain "the holiness without which no one may see the Lord" is not an easy work. It requires extensive conversion for us wherein the Lord, by the power of His cross, puts sins to death and raises grace to life. We must die to sin so that Christ may live in us. And there are many who simply do not want to follow this path since it involves giving up some of their favorite sins. They reject the kingdom of God because they love the world too much. The process of conversion from the things of this world to God is arduous at times and involves substantial effort. Many, knowing this implicitly, reject the call and the promise that grace can make all things possible. The road to heaven is narrow because it is the way of the cross, and too many do not want to hear about crosses or sacrifices of any sort.

It is in this context that the doctrine of hell makes the most sense. Hell exists because God respects the freedom of every individual to accept or reject His offer of the kingdom. For the reasons just stated and others we will explore in this book, many do not want to traverse the narrow road to the promised land of heaven. They are like the Hebrews in the time of Moses who preferred to remain in the desert rather than battle for the Promised Land. For them, it was too much trouble. Hence, God let them tarry in the desert. If they didn't want the Promised Land, God would not force them to enter it. Only those like Joshua and Caleb who desired it and were willing to take the narrow road lived to see it.

It is a caricature of the doctrine of hell to say that it exists because a mean and hateful God seeks to keep people out. No, hell exists because God respects our freedom to accept or reject Him and His kingdom. The nature of the judgment is this: that the Light has come into the world, but many prefer the darkness.

It may well be that many who reject the doctrine of hell today do so more as the rejection of the caricature of it than because they have thoughtfully reviewed the teaching. The purpose of this book is to ponder the doctrine and explain why it makes sense and is, in fact, a necessary doctrine if human beings exercise free will. The approach here is not so much a heavy theological or historical approach that seeks to review what every council, pope, Church Father, or saint ever said about hell. Neither does it seek to directly sample and refute, point by point, every argument by those who say hell is empty. Rather, this book seeks to respond to the questions, misunderstandings, and doubts pastorally and biblically about hell that average people today are raising. Such an approach will necessarily focus on human freedom, taking seriously the dignity and responsibility that such freedom confers. We are free to choose, but we are not free not to choose. Choose wisely, dear reader, and courageously, realizing that while salvation is freely offered, discipleship is costly and traverses the narrow road of the cross. Ask for a heart that is so touched by the glory of God and the joys unspeakable of heaven that no sacrifice is too great to say yes to God, joyfully let Him go to work, doing whatever is necessary to prepare us for the glories untold that await us.

CHAPTER 1

The Most Widespread of Heresies

The Denial of the Dogma of Hell

I would not be a sinner,
I'll tell you the reason why,
I'm afraid my Lord might call my name,
And I wouldn't be ready to die.

—African-American Spiritual

Many people believe hell is incompatible with the idea of a loving God. But Jesus combines them! Here is an important truth: *No one loves you more than Jesus Christ, yet no one spoke of or taught on hell and judgment more than He did.* He gave urgent warning after warning in parable after parable about final judgment and the reality of hell.

No "heresy" of our day is more widespread or pernicious than the denial of hell, its existence, and the sad truth that many go there. Here, the word *heresy* is not used in a formal way but in a broad, more descriptive sense that simply means picking and choosing among revealed truths. Strictly speaking, heresy would be the claim that there is no hell at all. What is more common today, at least among the faithful, is not the outright denial of hell but a kind of practical denial of it by concluding, contrary to Scripture, that very few, if any, go to hell. Confronted with truths that are in some tension (such as God's justice vs. His mercy or human freedom vs. God's sovereignty), the "heretic" chooses one truth and throws out the other to resolve the tension. While orthodoxy accepts both, heresy picks one and discards the other.

This book will not quote extensively from authors who argue that the vast majority are saved or that hell is largely empty. However, it will discuss three basic objections to the teaching of Matthew 7:13 that many are lost and few are saved. Some say it offends against God's love. Others say that human knowledge or understanding is too limited to make damnable choices. Still others argue that human freedom is too diminished to be fully accountable for choices made. Let's take a brief look at each claim.

Is Hell Irreconcilable with God's Love and Mercy?

With respect to the teaching on hell and judgment, the "heretic" cannot reconcile God's love and mercy with the reality of hell and eternal separation from Him. To him, it seems a contradiction, and so he largely sets aside the reality of hell, relegating it to the rarest of outcomes, reserved only for the most wicked sinner. Conflict resolved, or so he thinks. The problem is that both truths are taught and both truths must be held. God is Love and there is also a hell of which the loving Lord warns that many, not few, go there (see, e.g., Mt 7:13). Since truth cannot contradict itself, the conflict between love and hell is only apparent, and it falls to us to resolve it.

Let us be clear: no one loves you or me more than Jesus, and yet the Lord of Love, Jesus, spoke of these truths more than anyone else. The Church teachings on hell and the drama of the judgment that awaits us are largely taken from the very words of Jesus. He combines a keen sense of the need to repent or to risk hell with His love and desire to save us. If we see a contradiction between these truths, the problem is with our perception. These doctrines as taught by the Church are coherent and harmonious. Hence, any conflict between God's love and the existence of hell is an apparent conflict, not a real one.

Are Most People "Too Stupid" to Go to Hell?

Others are dismissive of hell by holding that most human beings do not have sufficient knowledge of God and what God requires to merit hell. While invincible ignorance can lessen guilt, as these critics suggest, it does not amount to a blank check. Even those who have not been catechized or taught the Christian faith still have intellect and will. They also have consciences and hearts wherein God has written His name and placed the natural law, which is discoverable by reason and which must be followed. St. Paul makes this clear about the Gentiles, who, though they did not have the Scriptures, were without excuse: "For what can be known about God is plain to them, because God has shown it to them. Ever since the creation of the world his invisible nature, namely, his eternal power and deity, has been clearly perceived in the things that have been made. So they are without excuse" (Rom 1:19–20).

St. Paul goes on to accuse them of suppressing the truth and, through the darkened intellect and depraved mind, engaging in every sort of sinful practice and sexual perversion (see Rom 21ff). So, even though they lacked the advantages of the Jews, who had Sacred Scripture, they were still responsible for what they knew by the natural law and were without excuse. St. Paul concludes of them: "Though they know God's decree that those who do such things deserve to die, they not only do them but approve those who practice them" (Rom 1:32).

Hence, while accepting that invincible ignorance can be a factor that God will account for in His judgment of us, God Himself, in His own word, teaches us that ignorance, especially of basic moral norms, is not as deep or widespread as many modern theologians may assume. Deep down, most people know what they are doing and if it is right or wrong. God's moral law is written in the human heart and in the "Book of Creation." Emphasizing ignorance or insufficient knowledge sets aside biblical norms that presume sufficient knowledge in general. Modern notions of widespread ignorance also diminish human dignity when they presume that many, if not most, are "too stupid" to go to hell. The assertion here is that God's word says otherwise, ascribing to human beings sufficient intellect, conscience, and will to be moral agents responsible for what they do.

Do People Lack Sufficient Freedom to Go to Hell?

Still others are dubious of there being "many" in hell due to factors that limit human freedom. There are, in fact, things that limit human freedom to a sufficient degree as to lower the culpability (blameworthiness) of sin. Bad habits, compulsions, and addictions may mean that mortal sins rank more as venial sins in some individuals. God, who is just and knows the heart, will surely account for such factors. So, do most lack sufficient freedom to deserve hell?

The answer to this question must ultimately be no. If not, the entire moral exhortation of the Scriptures would be quite pointless, and its warnings of the consequences of sin would be downright cruel. The stance of God and His Scripture, as well as that of the Church, is to engage the human person as a moral agent who can freely choose, making decisions for which he is responsible.

While the Church does teach that freedom can experience certain limits that lessen moral culpability, this teaching ought not be over-applied. The tone and tenor of Scripture tell us to teach God's law and insist upon it, warning of the consequences of unrepentant rebellion. There is no general qualifier attached to most biblical warnings, to wit: "But don't worry too much about the consequences of sins mentioned here since most of you aren't free enough to actually commit a mortal sin." Hence, while not wholly disregarding diminished freedom in certain cases, we ought not apply exculpatory language in excess of what God Himself does. God treats us as moral agents and in a way that generally assumes we possess sufficient freedom to make individual choices that can also

build to existential choices. Jesus warns of hell because it is a
real possibility. The Church should do no less.

Come to Your Senses

For these and other reasons, we moderns too easily refuse to
obey what is taught in Scripture. We refuse to accept that the
choices we make ultimately matter. We have been bewitched
by the fairy-tale ending that everyone "lived happily ever
after." We deny that the sum of our choices constitutes our
character and that our character ushers in our chosen destiny. We refuse to take responsibility for the fact that *we*
make consequential choices that build over time. Instead, we
blame God and accuse *Him* (who sent His own Son to save
us) of being wrong; we say that *He* is responsible for whether
we go to hell or not. Meanwhile, God is pleading, "Come to
me, before it is finally time to rise and close the door!"

We need to be sober about this; Jesus certainly was. He
warned and warned and warned; He pleaded and pleaded
and pleaded. He knows whereof we are made; He knows
how stubborn and stiff-necked we are, that we don't like
being told what to do. Yes, Jesus sadly observed that many
prefer the darkness to the light. Was He wrong in His judgment about us as individuals or as a human race? Surely
not. His diagnosis of our spiritual condition should be
taken seriously.

Are we smarter or holier than St. Paul, who, taking Jesus's
urgent warnings seriously, admonished: "Therefore, my
beloved, as you have always obeyed, so now, not only as in
my presence but much more in my absence, work out your

own salvation with fear and trembling" (Phil 2:12)? Was St. Paul too anxious when he said of himself, "I discipline my body and make it my slave, so that after I have preached to others, I myself will not be disqualified" (1 Cor 9:27)?

What of the countless saints who have warned the faithful of the ever-present dangers and woes of hell? What of they who had visions of hell and the numerous souls there? What of our Blessed Mother, who both warned of hell and even showed the children of Fatima its awful reality?

Can we really dismiss such testimonies, warnings, and revelations of our Lord, our Lady, and the saints about judgment and damnation as merely distant and rare possibilities that could not apply to the vast majority of us? Were they wrong? Were they simply seeking to scare us or manipulate us? Do we know better than they did?

If we honestly assess all this evidence, as this book will seek to do, we should admit that our current and modern view is at extreme odds with the testimony of Scripture, the tradition, and that of the saints. This need not scare us, but it should sober and humble us.

As we reconsider the modern view of improbable damnation and hell, we should surely begin with our Lord Himself, and we will discover that He devoted substantial teaching and frequent warnings about hell. As we shall see in the next chapter, His warnings on this matter are substantial and urgent.

CHAPTER 2

Why Hell Has to Be

You Are Free to Choose, but You Are Not Free Not to Choose

A man once gave a great banquet, and invited many. . . . But they all alike began to make excuses. The first said to him, "I have bought a field, and I must go out and see it; I pray you, have me excused." And another said, "I have bought five yoke of oxen, and I go to examine them; I pray you, have me excused." And another said, "I have married a wife, and therefore I cannot come."

—Luke 14:16, 18–20

Hell has to be. Frequently, those who doubt Jesus's biblical teaching ask this: If God is love, then why is there hell, and why is it eternal?

God's Respect for Our Freedom

In short, there is hell because of God's respect for our freedom. God made us free, and our freedom is absolutely necessary if we are to love. Suppose that a young man wanted a young lady to love him. Suppose again that he found a magic potion with which to lace her drink. After drinking

8

it, presto, she "loves" him! Is it real love? No, it's the effect of chemicals. Love must be freely given. The yes of love is only meaningful if we are free to say no. God invites us to love Him. There must be a hell because there must be a real alternative to heaven. God will not force us to love Him or to come to heaven with Him.

With this in mind, consider that God is very serious about the freedom He granted us, so much so that many grow angry when He does not quickly intervene in human affairs where there is great injustice or human tragedy. In our times, for instance, it is astonishing to many people that God has not intervened to stop abortion, that He did not end the Holocaust immediately, or that He has permitted so many cruel evils and crises to go unchecked. But, with rare exceptions, God does not force us to obey His law. As already noted, freedom is necessary for there to be love. The physical world must follow physical laws, animals follow instincts, but the human person is free because we are summoned to be sons and daughters of God, not slaves, or animals, or things. This is our dignity, along with the angels, that we are free, and this freedom allows us to love and accept God on His terms, or not. And, for freedom to be a true freedom, there must be real alternatives to what God offers. This is why there was the Tree of the Knowledge of Good and Evil in the Garden of Eden. Of this tree, it is said, "it was good for food and pleasing to the eyes, and it was desirable for obtaining wisdom" (Gn 3:6). Freedom is not true freedom where the alternatives to what is offered are undesirable or just plain awful.

Hence, we currently live in a world with its charms and desirable things. God warns us, as He did of the Tree with Adam and Eve, that these finite pleasures are not the answer to our infinite longing. And His warnings and teachings are on every page of Scripture, in the mouths of prophets and teachers, and from the heart and teaching of His own Son in the Gospels and in the Church's theology. Simply put, we cannot serve two masters, we cannot serve God and "mammon" (cf. Mt 6:24). We are free to choose, but we are not free not to choose. And "many" clearly choose mammon (worldly riches). "Fewer" choose God and His heavenly kingdom, if we are to take the words of Jesus seriously. More on this in a moment, but note here that, because of His respect for our freedom, God does not simply overrule our choices. He surely sends us graces and reminders; He never stops calling until our decision becomes final. But here is the point: we are free. It really is for us to choose heaven, or not. Jesus urgently sought to remind us of this in His teachings and the call to discipleship: "Repent and believe the gospel!" The freedom to answer this call is our dignity and a necessary aspect of our vocation to love.

Heaven Is What It Is

But wait a minute; doesn't everyone want to go to heaven? Yes, but it is often a "heaven" as they define it, not the real heaven. Many people understand heaven egocentrically: it's a place where they will be happy on their own terms, where what pleases them will be available in abundance. The real heaven is the kingdom of God in all its fullness. So while everyone wants to go to a "heaven" as they define it, not everyone wants to live in the real heavenly kingdom of God. Consider the following examples:

- **The kingdom of God is about mercy and forgiveness.** But not everyone wants to show mercy or forgiveness. Some prefer revenge. Others favor severe justice. Some prefer to cling to their anger and nurse resentments or bigotry. Further, not everyone wants to receive mercy and forgiveness. Some cannot possibly fathom why anyone would need to forgive them since they are right! Recall the second son in the parable of the prodigal son. Instead of entering the feast at the pleading of his father, he refuses to enter because that wretched brother of his is in there. He will not forgive or love his brother as the father does. In so doing, he excludes himself from the feast. Despite his father's pleading, he will not enter through forgiveness and mercy. The feast is not a feast at all for him. Similarly, heaven will not be "heaven" for those who refuse the grace to forgive and love their enemies and those who have harmed them.

- **The kingdom of God is about chastity.** God is very clear with us that His kingdom values chastity. For the unmarried, this means no genital sexual contact. For the married, this means complete fidelity to each other. Further, things such as pornography, lewd conduct, and immodesty are excluded from the kingdom. Many people today do not prefer chastity. They would rather be unchaste and immodest. Many celebrate fornication and homosexual acts as a kind of liberation from "repressive" norms. Many people like to consume pornography and do not want to limit their sexual conduct. It is one thing to fail in some of these matters through weakness, but it is quite another to defiantly insist that there is nothing wrong with such behavior.

- **The kingdom of God is about liturgy.** All of the descriptions of heaven emphasize liturgy. There are hymns being sung. There is the praise of God. There is standing, sitting, and prostrating at certain times. There are candles, incense, and long robes. There is a scroll or book that is opened, read, and appreciated. There is the Lamb on a throne-like altar. It's all very much like the Mass—but many are not interested in such things. They stay away because they say it's "boring." Perhaps they don't like the hymns and all the praise. Perhaps the scroll (the Lectionary) and its contents do not interest them or agree with their moral preferences. Having God at the center rather than themselves is unappealing.

This is the point: if heaven isn't just of our own design, if the real heaven of the kingdom of God is about these things, then it becomes clear that there are many who may not want to go to heaven as it is. Yes, everyone wants to go to a "heaven" of their own design, but not everyone wants to live in the real kingdom of heaven. God will not force anyone to live in heaven. He will not force anyone to love Him or what He loves or whom He loves. We are free to choose His kingdom or not.

Consider here the image of the father in the parable of the prodigal son. He is pleading with his second son to enter the feast for the returned son. But this second son does not want to enter on account of his brother's presence. And thus, the heavenly Father calls, but He does not force. It is a sad but simple fact that many prefer the darkness of this world to the light of God (cf. Jn 3:19).

A Brief Story to Illustrate the Point

I once knew a woman in one of my parishes who, in many ways, was very devout. She went to daily Mass and prayed the Rosary on most days. There was one thing about her, however, that was very troubling: she disliked African Americans.

She would often comment to me, "I can't stand Black people! They're moving into this neighborhood and ruining everything! I wish they'd go away." I remember scolding her a number of times for this sort of talk, but it seemed to have no effect.

One day, I decided to try to make it clearer. I said to her, "You know, you don't really want to go to heaven." "Of course I do, Father!" she replied. "God and the Blessed Mother are there; I want to go!" "No, you won't be happy there at all," I responded. "Why?" she asked, "What are you talking about, Father?" "Well, you see, there are Black people in heaven, and you've said that you can't stand to be around them, so I'm afraid you wouldn't be happy there. But don't worry, God won't force you to live in heaven if you won't be happy there. That's why I think that you don't really want to go to heaven." I think she got the message because I noticed that her attitude started to improve.

That's just it, isn't it? God will not force us to live in the kingdom if we really don't want it or like what that kingdom is. But we can't just invent our own "heaven." Heaven is a real place. It has contours and realities of its own that we can't just brush aside. Either we accept heaven as it is or *ipso facto* we choose to live apart from it and God.

It is a sad but simple fact that many prefer the darkness of this world to the light of God (cf. Jn 3:19). This is very obvious today, where many openly defy many of the teachings of God and the values of His kingdom. Many of His teachings are scorned by vast numbers as intolerant, unreasonable, outdated, and even hateful. Many, indeed, hate the truth and thus see the truth as hateful. God sends graces and messengers of His truth, but He does not force compliance. For those who die unrepentant, God grants them, it would seem, a place apart where the darkness they prefer and the sins they cling to are present in abundance (see Jn 3:19–21). It is not a pleasant place, but it is what they want in the place of the real heaven. In the end, you get what you want, and it is a sad reality that many (not few) do not want what God is offering. To some extent, heaven is an acquired taste and God must heal our worldly wounded hearts to desire what He offers. Sadly, only few (not many) are willing to let Him do this heart surgery. Be among that few!

Hell Really Does Exist

God permits people to live apart from Him and sadly teaches that many prefer other things to Him or to the real heaven. While hell is not a pleasant place, the saddest thing about the souls who go there is that they wouldn't be happy in heaven anyway. It's a tragic plight, not to be happy anywhere.

Understand this too. As we shall read in another chapter, God has not utterly rejected even the souls in hell. Somehow, He still provides for their basic needs. They continue to exist, and thus God continues to sustain them with whatever is required for that existence. He does not annihilate them or snuff them out.

But God *does* respect their wish to live apart from the kingdom and its values. He loves them but respects their choice.

A Thought from C. S. Lewis

In his book *The Great Divorce*, C. S. Lewis makes this very point. In it, a number of people ride a bus up from hell to "tour" heaven. Most of them do not like what they find. Some struggle to adjust to its brightness or its "weightiness." And many of the examples in the book are subtle since they do not feature violently evil people. For example, one man grows angry when he sees that the one who murdered his friend had repented and was in heaven. He finds such mercy too much to endure. Angry, he returns to the bus that goes back to hell rather than to acknowledge the glory of mercy and his own need to humbly repent. Another man, a former priest and theologian, prefers to return to hell when he discovers that dissent and theological debate are not part of heaven, only the firm clarity of truth. He feels too superior and "tolerant" to abide the excessive certainty of citizens of heaven and also insists on returning to hell. And there are many other similar stories where the bus riders from hell cannot accept that heaven is something other than what they think it should be. When their tour of heaven ended, most returned to hell.

Yes, hell has to be. You and I really are free to choose, but we are not free not to choose. God respects our freedom, but freedom presupposes a choice that must be made. Hell is ultimately about our freedom and summons to love. It's about the real heaven. It's about what we really want in the end. The Lord Himself laments that, though the Light has come into the world, many prefer the darkness. We know what God wants: to save us! The real judgment in question is what we want.

Having established the "need" for hell on account of God's respect for our freedom, we now turn to Jesus's urgent call for us to decide well. Jesus persistently taught on the urgent drama before us all. Heaven is open to us, but do we really want what God is offering? In His love for us, and His desire for us to choose wisely, Jesus spoke volumes on the judgment before us and the "binary" truth that the light of heaven is offered but too many prefer the darkness of hell. In the next chapter, we survey His urgent call and voluminous warnings.

CHAPTER 3

Jesus's Consistent Theme

A Survey of Jesus's Teachings and Warnings on Judgment and Hell

For whoever is ashamed of me and of my words,
of him will the Son of man be ashamed
when he comes in his glory
and the glory of the Father
and of the holy angels.

—Luke 9:26

To those who consider it untenable that a just and loving God would allow many to be lost and comparatively few saved, there is a predictable response: Jesus never got the memo. As we shall see, when directly asked if many or few will be saved, Jesus said few. In future chapters, we will discuss why this might be so. But first we should review and thereby demonstrate that Jesus consistently taught and warned of the coming judgment faced by all and warned that many, not few, would be lost and excluded from the kingdom of heaven. The texts are many, so many in fact that not all of them can be included here. But, as this compilation will show, those who deny hell or consider it a rare possibility must reject a huge number of biblical texts in order to do so. We should also recall that no one loves us more than Jesus, yet no one warned of judgment and hell more than He did, *no one*. An old spiritual captures succinctly the Gospel message: *Softly and tenderly Jesus is calling, calling "O Sinner, come home!"* He does not teach this merely to scare us but to sober and truthfully tell us that we are in a battle for souls, beginning with our own. Listen then in love and faith. We need a savior, but He needs our "yes."

Here, then, are many texts that warn of hell; most of them are right from the mouth of Jesus. A brief commentary follows each text. Take note that many of the sins and attitudes described below that can lead to hell if unrepented are ordinary things. They are not only the most serious offences like murder, rape, kidnapping and so forth.

Matthew 7:13

Jesus said, "Enter by the narrow gate. For the gate is wide and the way is easy that leads to destruction, and those who enter by it are many. For the gate is narrow and the way is hard that leads to life, and those who find it are few."

Do you understand this? More are lost than are saved. This is a startling text in terms of its sweeping quality. Some might ask why God would permit this. However, the meaning of the text is clear: many (not few) are lost. Hear Jesus's pleading and be sober about how stubborn and stiff-necked we can be. Why is the way narrow and hard? Because it is the way of the cross, and most people do not want the way of the cross. They prefer the immediate pleasures of sin and this world to the harder path of resisting temptation and reaching for a higher and ultimate glory in heaven. There is an old saying, "One bird in the hand is worth two in the bush." In other words, I prefer to hang on to the one bird I currently have than to go through the trouble of catching two more hard-to-reach birds. It's just too much trouble. Immediate pleasure outweighs future blessings, no matter how much we are told these distant blessings are far greater. Having to wait or go to any effort is a form of suffering similar though not identical to the cross. And the cross is the narrow and hard way. Many, not few, prefer the easy and broad way of the world's more immediate blessings. What follows in the next passage is a version from Luke's Gospel.

Luke 13:22–30

And some one said to him, "Lord, will those who are saved be few?" And he said to them, "Strive to enter by the narrow door; for many, I tell you, will seek to enter and will not be able. When once the householder has risen up and shut the door, you will begin to stand outside and to knock at the door, saying, 'Lord, open to us.' He will answer you, 'I do not know where you come from.' Then you will begin to say, 'We ate and drank in your presence, and you taught in our streets.' But he will say, 'I tell you, I do not know where you come from; depart from me, all you workers of iniquity!' There you will weep and gnash your teeth, when you see Abraham and Isaac and Jacob and all the prophets in the kingdom of God and you yourselves thrust out. And men will come from east and west, and from north and

*south, and sit at table in the kingdom of God. And behold, some
are last who will be first, and some are first who will be last."*

Here Jesus develops the teaching a bit that the blessings of
this world are pyrrhic. They are temporary victories won at
too high a cost. Elsewhere Jesus warns, "What does it profit
a man to gain the whole world, yet lose or forfeit his very
self?" (Lk 9:25).

The protest of those excluded in this passage is rooted
in the error that one can want and have the world's immediate blessings and also want the kingdom of God and its
blessings. But the Lord teaches elsewhere that a friend of
this world makes himself an enemy to God and His kingdom (see Jas 4:4). If a man who finds values such as love of
one's enemy, chastity, or forgiveness "too hard" or even silly,
old-fashioned, and unrealistic, will he suddenly desire them
at death? This is not how our hearts work. The kingdom of
heaven is an acquired taste that takes time to develop. And
while those excluded seem to want in, they don't really know
what they are asking and that they would be more miserable
in heaven than hell. This is the very sad end of those who
prefer darkness to light and the world to the kingdom of
God. The light of heaven is too bright, and its values obnoxious to them. In a way, the Lord spares them and says, "I
know you not, nor do I know the kind of world you come
from or prefer. Depart from me, this kingdom is not for you.
You'd just be miserable."

The fundamental question for us is: Do I want what God
is offering or not?

Matthew 5:22

But I say to you that every one who is angry with his brother shall be liable to judgment; whoever insults his brother shall be liable to the council, and whoever says, 'You fool!' shall be liable to the hell of fire.

Even unrighteous anger, unrepented of, is damnable behavior. We tend to justify our anger; God does not. He warns that we cannot cling to it and still enter heaven.

Matthew 5:29–30

If your right eye causes you to sin, pluck it out and throw it away; it is better that you lose one of your members than that your whole body be thrown into hell. And if your right hand causes you to sin, cut it off and throw it away; it is better that you lose one of your members than that your whole body go into hell.

The context here is sexual sin. We make light of this more than other sins, but the Lord does not. He is not saying that we should mutilate ourselves but rather that it is more serious to sin than to lose our eye, foot, or hand. We do not think this way, but God does. He warns us that our most serious problem is not our physical health or finances or any other passing concern; our most serious problem is our sin and the damage it can cause. Heed well the cost of sexual sin and other serious sins. Repent, or it may cost you your soul and the eternal life which the Lord offers.

Matthew 6:14–15

For if you forgive others their trespasses, your heavenly Father will also forgive you, but if you do not forgive others their trespasses, neither will your Father forgive your trespasses.

This is a pretty clear warning that we must allow God to give us the grace of mercy and forgiveness or else we cannot enter heaven. There is a kind of mathematics to the kingdom that is behind this teaching which says, "The measure that you measure to others will be measured back to you" (Mt 7:2). Blessed are the merciful, for (only) they will obtain mercy (Mt 5:7). St. James also warns, "For judgment is without mercy to one who has shown no mercy" (Jas 2:13). Hence, to be unnecessarily harsh in our punishments or judgments of others will result in a harsh standard of judgment being used by God toward us. Wherever, and to whatever degree possible, we should show mercy since we will need mercy shown to us on the day of judgment. Beware!

Luke 12:4–5

I tell you, my friends, do not fear those who kill the body, and after that have nothing more that they can do. But I will warn you whom to fear: fear him who, after he has killed, has authority to cast into hell. Yes, I tell you, fear him!

Many think that Jesus is talking about the devil here. But nowhere are we told to fear the devil; rather, we are to resist him. Further, the devil has no authority to judge us or to cast us into hell. Only Jesus has this authority. Yes, He will judge us, as is written, "For the Father judges no one, but has given all judgment to the Son, that all may honor the Son, just as they honor the Father" (Jn 5:22–23). Many today have tended to trivialize Jesus and reduce Him to a kind of harmless hippie. No indeed; He is the Lord. He loves us but expects to be taken seriously, to be revered, to be regarded with a holy and reverential fear, for as He says, He has the power to cast into hell. Yet, too often we fear man and the world more than we fear the Lord. This is no way to be ready for judgment. Our main concern should always be with what pleases the Lord. Too often what the Lord wants is the least of our concerns. But St. Paul tells us the Lord Jesus will be our judge: "So . . . we make it our aim to please him. For we must all appear before the judgment seat of Christ, so that each one may receive what is due for what he has done in the body, whether good or evil" (2 Cor 5:9–10).

Matthew 11:21–24

Woe to you, Chorazin! Woe to you, Bethsaida! For if the mighty works done in you had been done in Tyre and Sidon, they would have repented long ago in sackcloth and ashes. But I tell you, it will be more bearable on the day of judgment for Tyre and Sidon than for you. And you, Capernaum, will you be exalted to heaven? You will be brought down to hell. For if the mighty works done in you had been done in Sodom, it would have remained until this day. But I tell you that it will be more tolerable on the day of judgment for the land of Sodom than for you.

The people of these ancient cities were under a sentence of coming condemnation for their lack of faith. Despite grace and the evidence of many signs and miracles, they did not repent. If this does not change at once, they are under sentence of hell. Don't think that just because you're a member of "the club," you've got it made. Indeed, for those who have heard and seen, more is required, not less. A refusal to receive and show forth the obedience of faith (see Rom 1:5; 16:26) is a path of stubbornness that leads inevitably to hell.

Matthew 12:36–37

I tell you, on the day of judgment people will give account for every careless word they speak, for by your words you will be justified, and by your words you will be condemned.

While it is true that there can be a matter of light gossip or banter, too easily do we carelessly ruin reputations and reveal things that scandalize children or others. In the more serious of these matters, we risk the judgment of condemnation. Yes, we will have to give an account even for the least offensive gossip. Lord, have mercy!

Mark 9:42–48
(Giving Scandal)

Whoever causes one of these little ones who believe in me to sin, it would be better for him if a great millstone were hung around his neck and he were thrown into the sea. And if your hand causes you to sin, cut it off. It is better for you to enter life crippled than with two hands to go to hell, to the unquenchable fire. And if your foot causes you to sin, cut it off. It is better for you to enter life lame than with two feet to be thrown into hell. And if your eye causes you to sin, tear it out. It is better for you

to enter the kingdom of God with one eye than with two eyes to
be thrown into hell, "where their worm does not die and the fire
is not quenched."

This related teaching is clear enough: those who lead others
to sin are going to have to answer to Jesus for what they
have done. Note that "little ones" here does not merely mean
children. Jesus uses this term for all His disciples, young and
old. It is a damnable sin to lead others into sin, and Jesus
insists on strong measures to prevent giving such scandal.
Sadly, there are many who celebrate sin, exult it in the cin-
ema, on the internet, and in literature, and make light of its
effect on the souls of millions. So serious is this that the Lord
says it is better to lose an eye, a hand, or foot than to do such
an awful thing. And while we are not permitted to literally
maim ourselves, we must take seriously the giving of scandal
or exposing ourselves to scandal, even if it means extensive
things like heavily restricting or "cutting off" the internet,
refusing to view or recommend bad films, ending sinful relationships and illicit sexual activity, and seriously curbing our
tongue. Otherwise, hellfire can be our lot.

John 3:19–21

And this is the judgment, that the light has come into the world,
and men loved darkness rather than light, because their deeds
were evil. For every one who does evil hates the light, and does
not come to the light, lest his deeds should be exposed. But he
who does what is true comes to the light, that it may be clearly
seen that his deeds have been wrought in God.

More will be said of these verses in another chapter, but note here that Jesus indicates a prime reason that many are condemned: they prefer the darkness. Hence, consigning people to hell ought not be ascribed to an angry, vengeful God. Rather, the judgment is a recognition by the Lord that many prefer the darkness to the light of God's glory and truth in heaven. Those who hate the truth often call the truth hateful. And those who prefer the darkness consider the light to be harsh. But, of course, the truth is not hateful, neither is the light harsh. Rather, it is for us to accustom ourselves to the light or not. Either we will allow God to accomplish this acclimation in us to the light of heaven and the temperature of glory, or we will find the light and warmth of heaven intolerable. Preferring the darkness, the Lord consigns us to what we prefer.

John 8:21ff

Jesus said to them, "You are of this world; but I am not of this world. I told you that you would die in your sins, for unless you believe that I AM, you will die in your sins. . . . I have much to say about you and much to condemn you for, but he who sent me is true, and I declare to the world what I have heard from him."

So, their refusal to believe is a damnable sin. They will die in their sins. Many of the people in the Temple area that day, including their leaders, were not simply being asked to believe in Jesus without graces and signs. Jesus had given them four fundamental signs to show them who he was: Scripture (for the Lord fulfilled hundreds of prophecies about the Messiah), His many miracles, the testimony of St. John the Baptist, and the testimony of the Father in their hearts (see Jn 5:30–47 where the Lord details these signs). So, they were not being asked to believe in someone who just stepped out of the blue. He was well-attested to be the Messiah and Lord He claimed to be. Further, the heavenly Father sent them graces they refused to accept. Because of their resistance to the Father's grace, Jesus said that they had separated themselves from God: "Whoever is of God hears the words of God. The reason why you do not hear them is that you are not of God" (Jn 8:47). Hence, we are dealing here with men and women who have hardened their hearts and were stubbornly refusing to believe. For this, Jesus says, they will die in their sins if they do not repent. How many people today have also hardened their hearts and are both stubborn and defiant to the Lord and His teachings? Indeed, many glory in their sins and have little shame in excoriating the Scriptures and the Church, considering their view superior to the revealed word of God. To those who resist, this warning applies: "You will die in your sins, unless you believe that I AM."

John 12:48–50

He who rejects me and does not receive my sayings has a judge; the word that I have spoken will be his judge on the last day. For I have not spoken on my own authority; the Father who sent me has himself given me commandment what to say and what to speak. And I know that his commandment is eternal life. What I say, therefore, I say as the Father has bidden me.

Here, too, we bring judgment upon ourselves. We might wish to blame God, but at the end of the day, we show by our own disposition that we are not fit for heaven and would not be happy there because it is the full realization of many things we either detest or scoff at (e.g., love of our enemies, forgiveness, chastity, worship of God). These verses are especially for believers who have heard the word of God but will not heed it. "For it is time for judgment to begin at the household of God; and if it begins with us, what will be the outcome for those who do not obey the gospel of God?" And "If the righteous is scarcely saved, what will become of the ungodly and the sinner?" (1 Pt 4:16–18). Of course, all of us fall short in keeping the Lord's words fully, and for that, confession is a necessary remedy. But consider well that many openly defy the words and teachings of Holy Scripture and, out of this defiance, refuse to repent. Their number is legion, and their situation is grave if they do not abandon their prideful rejection of the Lord's teaching found in His revealed Word and in the natural law observed in creation. This is an especially ominous warning to those who have been raised in the Faith and who have drifted or, even worse, apostatized from the faith by formally rejecting some or all of it.

Matthew 23:33–34

You serpents, you brood of vipers, how are you to escape being sentenced to hell? Therefore I send you prophets and wise men and scribes, some of whom you will kill and crucify, and some you will flog in your synagogues and persecute from town to town.

God knows how stubborn we are. But persevering in His will to save us, He sends help such as prophets, wise men, the Church, and sacraments. Nevertheless, many still stubbornly refuse and even seek to limit the Word of God by ignoring, silencing, marginalizing, persecuting, and criminalizing those who announce it. A few even go so far as to kill the messengers. Jesus devotes a parable to this topic. He teaches here that those who stubbornly resist the work of God to save them by these means are subject to hell since they do not want the truth and justice offered by God. He offers many opportunities for salvation, but those who reject His help bring condemnation upon themselves.

The Parables

We turn now to some of the parables of Jesus that warn of the coming judgment and the exclusion of some from the kingdom. Arguably twenty-one of the thirty-eight parables deal with this theme. We cannot survey all of them, but the ones that follow demonstrate in a creative and often terrifying way that a judgment is upon us and that we have a decision to make. Delay is exceedingly dangerous, and there comes a moment when our decision becomes final.

Matthew 13:24–30
(The Parable of the Wheat and the Tares)

Another parable he put before them, saying, "The kingdom of heaven may be compared to a man who sowed good seed in his field; but while men were sleeping, his enemy came and sowed weeds among the wheat, and went away. So when the plants came up and bore grain, then the weeds appeared also. And the servants of the householder came and said to him, 'Sir, did you not sow good seed in your field? How then has it weeds?' He said to them, 'An enemy has done this.' The servants said to him, 'Then do you want us to go and gather them?' But he said, 'No; lest in gathering the weeds you root up the wheat along with them. Let both grow together until the harvest; and at harvest time I will tell the reapers, Gather the weeds first and bind them in bundles to be burned, but gather the wheat into my barn.'"

This parable emphasizes the patient mercy of the Lord. However, the Lord's patience cannot last forever. There *is* a day of judgment; perhaps not now, but it will come! People need time to repent; plus, rashly seeking to root out all evil may cause collateral damage, even to the righteous. But God's patience is directed to our salvation; it is not delayed for its own sake. He expects us to use this time to repent and change the way we live. It is delay combined with a warning that when the time of patience and mercy is over, there are some who will be gathered out of the kingdom and consigned to flames. Consider how shameful it will be to be lost after all this patience and grace has been extended to us!

Matthew 22:1-14
(The Parable of the Wedding Banquet)

And again Jesus spoke to them in parables, saying, "The kingdom of heaven may be compared to a king who gave a marriage feast for his son, and sent his servants to call those who were invited to the marriage feast; but they would not come. Again he sent other servants, saying, 'Tell those who are invited, Behold,

I have made ready my dinner, my oxen and my fat calves are killed, and everything is ready; come to the marriage feast.' But they made light of it and went off, one to his farm, another to his business, while the rest seized his servants, treated them shamefully, and killed them. The king was angry, and he sent his troops and destroyed those murderers and burned their city. Then he said to his servants, 'The wedding is ready, but those invited were not worthy. Go therefore to the thoroughfares, and invite to the marriage feast as many as you find.' And those servants went out into the streets and gathered all whom they found, both bad and good; so the wedding hall was filled with guests. "But when the king came in to look at the guests, he saw there a man who had no wedding garment; and he said to him, 'Friend, how did you get in here without a wedding garment?' And he was speechless. Then the king said to the attendants, 'Bind him hand and foot, and cast him into the outer darkness; there men will weep and gnash their teeth.' For many are called, but few are chosen."

Here is a shocking parable of a king who, in the end, accepts the "no" of the invited guests. However, through fearsome imagery, the Lord teaches that the alternative to the wedding feast is a fiery, destructive loss of everything. It is a truly shocking parable as we consider the angry king sending his army to destroy their town. God is not angry as we are, but to set ourselves in opposition to His will and invitation is to experience wrath within ourselves that we project on Him. More on this later. Take note that the fiery destruction of their town was, in fact, fulfilled in AD 70 when the Lord permitted the Roman Army to destroy Jerusalem and the temple. The Lord had given the invited guests forty biblical years to accept His invitation to the heavenly wedding banquet. But in the end, the only alternative for those who rejected the invitation was hellfire and the loss of everything.

In the parable, the call went to the Gentiles, many of whom did respond well to the invitation. But here also, one was found not wearing the proper wedding attire. This is the robe of righteousness (see Rv 7:14; 19:8; 22:14; Is 61:10; Col 3:12) in which God clothes His faithful. It is required that we accept this righteousness to be able to enter the kingdom of heaven. It is not as if God did not offer us the garment. Hence the man's refusal to wear it is not mere rudeness; it is a stubborn unrepentance, and this excludes him from heaven.

Clearly, there are many today who simply refuse the righteousness God offers them. They do not want holiness and reject many of the virtues associated with it, since it would involve giving up their favorite sins. Sadly, this is true of many. For this reason, many are called, but few are chosen.

Matthew 24:36–51
(The Parable of the Unknown Day and Hour)

But of that day and hour no one knows, not even the angels of heaven, nor the Son, but the Father only. As were the days of Noah, so will be the coming of the Son of man. For as in those days before the flood they were eating and drinking, marrying and giving in marriage, until the day when Noah entered the ark, and they did not know until the flood came and swept them all away, so will be the coming of the Son of man. Then two men will be in the field; one is taken and one is left. Two women will be grinding at the mill; one is taken and one is left. Watch therefore, for you do not know on what day your Lord is coming. But know this, that if the householder had known in what part of the night the thief was coming, he would have watched and would not have let his house be broken into. Therefore you also must be ready; for the Son of man is coming at an hour you do not expect. Who then is the faithful and wise servant, whom his master has set over his household, to give them their food at the proper time? Blessed is that servant whom his master when he comes will find so doing. Truly, I say to you, he will set him over all his possessions. But if that wicked servant says to himself, "My master is delayed," and begins to beat his fellow servants, and eats and drinks with the drunken, the master of that servant will come on a day when he does not expect him and at an hour he does not know, and will punish him, and put him with the hypocrites; there men will weep and gnash their teeth.

We have been warned, so delay is not an excuse. Tomorrow is not promised. Some say there is no God, while others say there is no hell, but those who say there is no hurry cause the most harm. It is most harmful because this claim can be subtle and disguise itself as prudence, tolerance, or patience. But in reality, it is a deadly tranquilizer. So many today are lulled into inaction by presumptive delay. They are, as Jesus says, busy about eating, drinking, marrying, sleeping, and working; anything but repenting. Even the sudden death of friends or loved ones does not rouse them to salutary conversion. Since we have been warned, procrastination is a sin and the longer we delay, the more serious the sin becomes and the less likely we will change and repent.

The Lord promises great reward for those who are found diligent in the works of justice and mercy. They act as those who know they will be accountable to Him. But there are others, many others, who cavalierly abuse the Lord's delay and use it as a pretext for all sorts of bad behaviors and injustice. They refuse to ponder how they will justify to the Lord what they have or have not done. Jesus fearsomely says they will be caught off guard, cut to pieces, and assigned a place where there will be wailing and gnashing of teeth. It is a tragic thing to misconstrue mercy and patience lovingly offered and turn it into a form of disrespect to the Lord who offers it. God is patient, but He is not weak or a pushover; He is not to be mocked or disrespected. No one who does this could ever enjoy heaven, where God is esteemed and glorified by the angels and saints. Take the Lord seriously.

Matthew 24:43-44
(The Parable of the Thief)

But know this, that if the householder had known in what part of the night the thief was coming, he would have watched and would not have let his house be broken into. Therefore you also must be ready; for the Son of man is coming at an hour you do not expect.

The Lord uses a shocking image of presenting himself as a thief. He cannot be a thief because everything we claim as our own belongs to God. But to those who see things as their own and insist on being the master of their lives, the Lord will seem to come as a thief to end their agenda and reclaim what is His. He will not be seen as a Lord coming to reward them with joys unspeakable and glories untold. Hence, they will be fearful and angry before him at the judgment seat. The Lord often speaks of their wailing and grinding of teeth.

Luke 12:42–46
(The Day and Hour Unknown)

And the Lord said, "Who then is the faithful and wise steward, whom his master will set over his household, to give them their portion of food at the proper time? Blessed is that servant whom his master when he comes will find so doing. Truly, I tell you, he will set him over all his possessions. But if that servant says to himself, 'My master is delayed in coming,' and begins to beat the menservants and the maidservants, and to eat and drink and get drunk, the master of that servant will come on a day when he does not expect him and at an hour he does not know, and will punish him, and put him with the unfaithful."

This parable contains a similar theme but deepens the warning against presumption. God's patience is directed to our salvation. People need time to repent. But if instead of seeking to reform one's life, a person does the opposite and uses God's delay as an opportunity to sin even more, the sin is compounded. Though patient and merciful, God will not be mocked. The Lord expects to be taken seriously. Note, too, that the malefactor described here is not only guilty of social sins such as abuse and exploitation of others. He is also guilty of more personal sins such as gluttony and drunkenness. So once again, the sins that can merit hell are personal vices as well as more serious crimes. Ordinary things, as well, can harden our heart against the values of the kingdom of God and against His people. We must not delay our conversion from such things, lest our heart harden in favor of the darkness.

Matthew 25:1-13
(The Parable of the Ten Virgins)

Then the kingdom of heaven shall be compared to ten maidens who took their lamps and went to meet the bridegroom. Five of them were foolish, and five were wise. For when the foolish took their lamps, they took no oil with them; but the wise took flasks of oil with their lamps. As the bridegroom was delayed, they all slumbered and slept. But at midnight there was a cry, "Behold, the bridegroom! Come out to meet him." Then all those maidens rose and trimmed their lamps. And the foolish said to the wise, "Give us some of your oil, for our lamps are going out." But the wise replied, "Perhaps there will not be enough for us and for you; go rather to the dealers and buy for yourselves." And while they went to buy, the bridegroom came, and those who were ready went in with him to the marriage feast; and the door was shut. Afterward the other maidens came also, saying, "Lord, lord, open to us." But he replied, "Truly, I say to you, I do not know you." Watch therefore, for you know neither the day nor the hour.

The groom in this passage delays his arrival, but not forever! The Lord also teaches here that we cannot borrow someone else's readiness or share our readiness with others. We have to be ready for ourselves. The foolish virgins missed the groom's arrival through their own careless neglect. They do not really know or respect the groom or other guests since they regard the wedding of such little importance that they don't bother to do their one job: be ready with lamps trimmed and burning when the groom arrives. The groom does not recognize them as wedding guests when they seek entrance since they have not behaved as wedding guests. When the Lord says He does not know them, this is not a denial of the Lord's omniscience. The "knowing" here is not intellectual knowing. It is the knowing of deep, intimate, personal experience which the Lord seeks to offer us and receive from us. Our souls are to be espoused to the Lord in a covenant akin to marriage. But the Lord offers this saving relationship, He does not impose it. He knocks at the door; He does not barge in (see Rv 3:20). Hence, there is a kind of turning of the tables on the five foolish bridesmaids and all who ignore His invitation. Those who ignore the Lord's knock, make light of it, and refuse to open will themselves knock and not be admitted or recognized.

Many people ignore or make light of the Lord's knock through the preaching of the Gospel and other means: His beauty in creation, the ringing of a church bell, an old Bible on the bookshelf or table, the Christmas carols in December, and so forth. God does not neglect to knock. An old spiritual says, "Somebody's knocking at your door. Oh sinner! Why don't you answer?" We must answer. And to refuse to answer is its own answer. God will not force his entrance. We must open from the inside or perish.

Matthew 25:26–30
(The Parable of the Talents [conclusion])

But his master answered him, "You wicked and slothful ser-
vant! You knew that I reap where I have not sowed, and gather
where I have not winnowed? Then you ought to have invested
my money with the bankers, and at my coming I should have
received what was my own with interest. So take the talent from
him, and give it to him who has the ten talents. For to every one
who has will more be given, and he will have abundance; but
from him who has not, even what he has will be taken away.
And cast the worthless servant into the outer darkness; there
men will weep and gnash their teeth."

We will have to reckon for what we have done and what we
have failed to do with our gifts. One of the paradoxes of life is
that if we want to keep something unto eternal life, we must
generously share it. There is an old saying, "You can't take it
with you, but you can send it on ahead." Jesus tells us to store
up treasure in heaven. We do not do this by sending it up in
a balloon. Rather, we store it up by giving it out, sharing it
generously with others. Scripture says that our good deeds go
with us (see Rv 14:13). Jesus also warns us, "For where your
treasure is, there your heart will be also" (Mt 6:21). Hence,
if our treasure is in heaven, our heart and desires will also
direct us there. But the man who buried his treasure in the
earth represents those in this world who bury their treasure
here. Hence, they desire the things of earth and not those of
heaven. And to those who think they can desire both, Jesus
says, "No one can serve two masters, for either he will hate
the one and love the other, or he will be devoted to the one

and despise the other. You cannot serve God and money" (Mt 6:24). So build your heart's desires in heaven by generously investing the wealth and talents He has given you. Be not like many who sadly cling to their treasures here, in effect burying them. They will see the Lord on judgment day as a thief and an unreasonable Lord whom they will not serve.

Matthew 25:41–46

(Sheep and Goats [conclusion])

Then he will say to those at his left hand, "Depart from me, you cursed, into the eternal fire prepared for the devil and his angels; for I was hungry and you gave me no food, I was thirsty and you gave me no drink, I was a stranger and you did not welcome me, naked and you did not clothe me, sick and in prison and you did not visit me." Then they also will answer, "Lord, when did we see thee hungry or thirsty or a stranger or naked or sick or in prison, and did not minister to thee?" Then he will answer them, "Truly, I say to you, as you did it not to one of the least of these, you did it not to me." And they will go away into eternal punishment, but the righteous into eternal life.

A serious neglect of the poor and needy can be a damnable sin. In our current cultural setting, this neglect can be a simple, straightforward neglect, or it can manifest itself as a diversion of this responsibility to government agencies or other large-scale charities. This is not always wrong, but we cannot wholly set aside our personal obligations to the poor and needy, the sick and suffering, especially those in our own families. Elsewhere, Scripture calls upon us to lay down our lives for our brothers. "If anyone with earthly possessions sees his brother in need, but withholds his compassion from him, how can the love of God abide in him?" (1 Jn 3:16–17). Here, too, we see that hell is not simply reserved for genocidal maniacs or mass murders. Neglect of the poor is, sadly, a more ordinary sin. Those who commit it may be "nice people" in every other respect, but in the end, the Lord teaches that serious neglect of the poor can merit hellfire.

Luke 16:19–31
(Lazarus and Dives)

There was a rich man, who was clothed in purple and fine linen and who feasted sumptuously every day. And at his gate lay a poor man named Lazarus, full of sores, who desired to be fed with what fell from the rich man's table; moreover the dogs came and licked his sores. The poor man died and was carried by the angels to Abraham's bosom. The rich man also died and was buried; and in Hades, being in torment, he lifted up his eyes, and saw Abraham far off and Lazarus in his bosom. And he called out, "Father Abraham, have mercy upon me, and send Lazarus to dip the end of his finger in water and cool my tongue; for I am in anguish in this flame." But Abraham said, "Son, remember that you in your lifetime received your good things, and Lazarus in like manner evil things; but now he is comforted here, and you are in anguish. And besides all this, between us and you a great chasm has been fixed, in order that those who would pass from here to you may not be able, and none may cross from there to us." And he said, "Then I beg you, father, to send him to my father's house, for I have five brothers, so that he may warn them, lest they also come into this place of torment."

But Abraham said, "They have Moses and the prophets; let them
hear them." And he said, "No, father Abraham; but if some one
goes to them from the dead, they will repent." He said to him,
"If they do not hear Moses and the prophets, neither will they be
convinced if some one should rise from the dead."

Here, too, contempt and indifference toward the poor is a
damnable sin. Notice also that there is no evidence that the
rich man tormented or directly abused Lazarus. His sin was
fundamentally one of indifference. This lands him in hell.

Note, too, that the rich man does not change after death.
He is locked into his patterns. He does not ask to come to
heaven; he wants Lazarus sent to hell. He still does not recognize Lazarus's dignity; he sees him as an errand boy. After
death, the rich man is miserable, but he cannot and will
not change. This teaching on our fixed character after death
explains why hell is eternal: after death, our will is fixed and we
will not change. More will be said of this in a future chapter.

Revelation 21:8; 22:12-16

But to the cowardly and unbelieving and abominable and mur-
derers and sexually immoral and sorcerers and idolaters and all
liars, their place will be in the lake that burns with fire and sulfur.
. . . "Look, I am coming soon!" says the Lord. "My reward is with
me, and I will give to each person according to what they have
done. I am the Alpha and the Omega, the First and the Last, the
Beginning and the End. Blessed are those who wash their robes,
that they may have the right to the tree of life and may go through
the gates into the city. Outside are the dogs, those who practice
magic arts, the sexually immoral, the murderers, the idolaters and

everyone who loves and practices falsehood. I, Jesus, have sent my angel to give you this testimony for the churches. I am the Root and the Offspring of David, and the bright Morning Star."

Jesus vividly describes sinners as dogs, cowards, and abominable (i.e., monstrous) liars. This is shocking language, but Jesus used it often. We are often dainty, but Jesus is not. He is urgent and more than willing to describe what unrepentant sinners become. But how are they cowards? They are cowards because they did not bravely resist the temptations of this world but chose the easier paths of pleasure and worldly approval and rewards.

While serious sins such as murder and witchcraft and idolatry are mentioned, notice that more common sins are included, such as sexual immorality and the spreading of lies, contrary to the truth of the Gospel. Vast indeed in our times are those who scoff at the teachings of the Lord and spread lies, especially about sexual matters, the sacredness of life, and Holy Matrimony. Of these, Scripture says, "Woe to those who call evil good and good evil, who put darkness for light and light for darkness" (Is 5:20). Do not be numbered among them, and do not listen to them. A lake of fire awaits especially those who mislead others, and they are many.

Matthew 3:12

His winnowing fork is in his hand, and he will clear his threshing floor, gathering his wheat into the barn and burning up the chaff with unquenchable fire.

John the Baptist speaks here with clarity and frankness.

Summary

There are surely more things which the Lord said on the matter of judgment and hell. But allow these examples to illustrate that this was no small theme of the Lord's teaching. His admonitions are frequent, at times quite urgent and even shocking. To adopt notions of a largely empty hell requires us to overlook an enormous amount of teaching that came, not from fear-mongering clergy, but right from the mouth of the Lord Jesus Himself. Quite plainly, Jesus says many (not few) are at real risk of hell and not only for unrepentant sins of a radically violent nature but far more "ordinary" sins and attitudes, such as pride, lies, giving scandal, lukewarmness, drunkenness, procrastination, and indifference to the poor, sick, and needy. Though many sins may admit of light matter, such as gossip, it is also true that gossip can become very serious if, as is sometimes the case, it harms or ruins the reputation of others or breeds contempt and insolence. And so too for other sins that may seem harmless but can grow to become very serious. If we make light of His teachings, we deceive ourselves, and the truth is not in us. These teachings require of us a sober acceptance and serious moral reflection. We often call "good" or "no big deal" what God calls sin. This amounts to a foolish defiance. Scripture counsels a better way: acceptance with sobriety that one day our decision to accept or reject God's offer of salvation will become final: "Do not say, 'I have sinned, yet what has happened to me?' for the LORD is slow to anger! Do not be so confident of forgiveness that you add sin upon sin. Do not say, 'His mercy is great; my many sins he will forgive.' For mercy and anger alike are with him; his wrath comes to rest on the wicked. Do not delay turning back to the LORD, do not put it off day after day!" (Sir 5:5–7).

The Teaching of the Apostles

Jesus also commissioned the apostles to preach, teach, govern, and sanctify in His name. He said, "He who hears you is hearing me" (see Lk 10:16). Therefore, we do well to sample a few texts from them on these matters, realizing that in hearing them, we hear the voice of Jesus.

Hebrews 12:14

Strive for peace with everyone, and for the holiness without which no one will see the Lord.

Only those who allow God to make them holy can endure the bright lights of the kingdom of God. This text also speaks well to us of the likely need for some purgation after we die. For the Lord has said we must be perfect as the heavenly Father is perfect (see Mt 5:48). This is not a threat; it is a promise. But most of us know that upon death, we are often far short of godly perfection. Hence, if we die in friendship and faithfulness to the Lord, He will "bring to completion the good work he has begun in us" (see Phil 1:6). And when this work is complete, the glory of heaven, with its joys unspeakable and glories untold, will be ours! Of this heaven, Scripture says, "But nothing unclean will ever enter it, nor anyone who does what is detestable or false, but only those who are written in the Lamb's book of life" (Rv 21:27). Only God can give us the perfection needed for heaven. Hence, we should run to Him with eager hearts and submit ourselves to what is necessary. Sadly, many are either uninterested or averse to the kind of work God must do. But the author of the Letter to the Hebrews bids us to strive with the Lord for this essential work.

Hebrews 13:4 (ESV)

Let marriage be held in honor among all, and let the marriage bed be undefiled, for God will judge the sexually immoral and adulterous.

The modern age has shredded marriage at every turn. Not only have we set aside its biblical definition, but many have usurped the privileges of the marriage bed through every form of sexual promiscuity. God has joined Holy Matrimony, sexual intimacy, and the begetting of children. But we have separated what God has joined and are reaping a tragic harvest of many consequences, such as cohabitation, sexually transmitted disease, abortion, rampant divorce, children who live apart from their fathers, sexual abuse and exploitation, sexual trafficking, and rampant sexual confusion. The destruction of marriage and the sexual confusion that arose in the wake of the sexual revolution are immense and involve many victims and perpetrators. Many have fallen through weakness. But there is also a large number who remain defiant to God's teachings about chastity and marriage. As we shall see in some of the following quotations, sexual sins are serious and can quickly exclude one from the kingdom of heaven if they are not repented of or are defiantly celebrated as is too often the case today.

1 Corinthians 6:9 (ESV)

Or do you not know that the unrighteous will not inherit the kingdom of God? Do not be deceived: neither the sexually immoral, nor idolaters, nor adulterers, nor men who practice homosexuality.

As noted, many in the modern world make light of sexual sins, but God does not. He warns that these sins render us incapable of enduring the bright lights of heaven because we "prefer the darkness" of lust and other sins (*cf.* Jn 3:18). Fornication, most commonly understood today as premarital sex, is considered by most to be normative and good. Homosexual acts are outright celebrated with "pride" days and so forth. Indeed, it *is* a terrible form of human pride that we should celebrate openly acts that God calls sin. The same goes for fornication and adultery. In the end, it is always pride and stubbornness that exclude one from God's kingdom.

It is one thing to struggle with temptations to sin and disordered affections, such as with sexuality or various addictions. Such struggles are honorable and make for sanctity. But it is something far different to throw off God's teachings, refuse to repent, and even sacrilegiously invoke God's approval while openly defying His written Word. Scripture says, "Those who say, 'I know him,' but do not keep his commandments are liars, and the truth is not in them. But whoever keeps his word, the love of God is truly perfected in him" (1 Jn 2:4–5).

Tragically, the number of those who openly defy God's word about marriage and human sexuality is vast today, and this should summon us to prayer for the conversion of sinners. For, as the quotation above says, if they do not repent, they will not inherit the kingdom of God, and hell will be their final destination.

Ephesians 5:3–7 (ESV)

But sexual immorality and all impurity or covetousness must not even be named among you, as is proper among saints. Let there be no filthiness nor foolish talk nor crude joking, which are out of place, but instead let there be thanksgiving. For you may be sure of this, that everyone who is sexually immoral or impure, or who is covetous (that is, an idolater), has no inheritance in the kingdom of Christ and God. Let no one deceive you with empty words, for because of these things the wrath of God comes upon the sons of disobedience. Therefore do not become partners with them.

Once again, God says that sexual sin excludes us from the kingdom of God. We may go to hell if we die unrepentant because it shows that we prefer the darkness and cannot stand the light. Note with sobriety the teaching: No one who is unrepentant of sexual misconduct has any inheritance in the kingdom. Some may have fallen through weakness, but repentance unlocks mercy. But woe to those who remain defiant. They are not going to like or be able to endure the brightness of heaven where chastity is celebrated.

Galatians 5:19–21 (ESV)

Now the works of the flesh are evident: sexual immorality, impurity, sensuality, idolatry, sorcery, enmity, strife, jealousy, fits of anger, rivalries, dissensions, divisions, envy, drunkenness, orgies, and things like these. I warn you, as I warned you before, that those who do such things will not inherit the kingdom of God.

Once again, these are not sins on par with genocidal hatred. They are ordinary sins and attitudes, most of which afflict all of us to some extent. And while some are more serious than others, all sins can become severe enough to put our physical welfare or the well-being of others in jeopardy. St. Paul warns that living a morally discordant life can become very serious, for not inheriting heaven means going to hell.

1 Corinthians 9:26-27

Well, I do not run aimlessly, I do not box as one beating the air; but I pommel my body and subdue it, lest after preaching to others I myself should be disqualified.

If even St. Paul realized he had to be sober, why not us? Even Paul did not presumptively conclude that disqualification was a remote possibility, why do many today act so confidently? St. Paul does not say that this is a minor possibility but rather that it is a possibility that requires him to strike blows at his flesh and enslave his passions. This is generally not the kind of talk that comes from someone who considers hell largely empty. Further, it is unlikely that St. Paul had in mind that he might be guilty of extreme unrepented sins such as murder or genocide. Rather, he must have in mind the more common sins and attitudes that plague us all, even preachers of the Gospel.

James 2:12-13

So speak and so act as those who are to be judged under the law of liberty. For judgment is without mercy to one who has shown no mercy; yet mercy triumphs over judgment.

As has been noted above, the standards of judgment we use for others are the standards the Lord will use for us. Yet, sadly, there are some who use unnecessarily harsh or rash standards of judgment and severity in punishments. They should realize they are storing up trouble for themselves at their personal judgment. It is true that judgments, corrections, and punishment must be made, but to rush to the most severe of punishments is not wise. Help us to show mercy, Lord, for the measure we measure to others will be measured back to us (see Mt 7:2).

Romans 2:3-11

Do you suppose, O man, that when you judge those who do such things and yet do them yourself, you will escape the judgment of God? Or do you presume upon the riches of his kindness and forbearance and patience? Do you not know that God's kindness is meant to lead you to repentance? But by your hard and impenitent heart you are storing up wrath for yourself on the day of wrath when God's righteous judgment will be revealed. For he will render to every man according to his works: to those who by patience in well-doing seek for glory and honor and immortality, he will give eternal life; but for those who are factious and do not obey the truth, but obey wickedness, there will be wrath and fury. There will be tribulation and distress for every human being who does evil, the Jew first and also the Greek, but glory and honor and peace for every one who does good, the Jew first and also the Greek. For God shows no partiality.

Notice that this passage is rich in its warnings about stubbornness and presumption. The text says these vices flow from self-seeking and the rejection of the truth by those preferring evil to good. So, we are judged by deeds, not by prerogatives or by being "better" than someone else or the member of a group or movement, or by being "on the right side of history," etc. If God is patient, it is not because He approves of our sins; it is because he wants to give us time to repent and get things together. To presumptively squander this offer is to regard God's gift lightly, even with contempt. God will ultimately judge us impartially by our deeds, not by some pedigree or whether we attained worldly honors. It is what we did and how we used the gifts and opportunities God gave us that we will be judged. We will speak of what is meant by the "wrath of God" later.

Philippians 2:12

Therefore, my beloved, as you have always obeyed, so now, not only as in my presence but much more in my absence, work out your own salvation with fear and trembling.

So again, St. Paul never seems to have gotten the memo that condemnation or hell is a remote possibility. If he had, why warn us to work at our salvation with fear and trembling? Some call fear unhealthy. But that is too absolute. Some fears are healthy and rational. St. Paul does not summon us to panic but rather to a sober and holy fear rooted in love and reverence of God and the desire to obtain what He offers.

Summary of the Epistles

Here, too, this is but a small selection of texts. Many more texts could be set forth that admonish us in strong terms that sinful habits, attitudes, and acts, unrepented, can and do lead to hell. Given the broad and rather common occurrence of the listed sins and attitudes, can we easily conclude that hell is all but empty? Though God is rich in mercy and willing to forgive, there are vast numbers who refuse to repent because they regard evil as good. Is their error in this regard excusable? Only God can make that final judgment. But since, through His prophets and apostles, God warns so clearly and persistently, we cannot feign total ignorance. Neither should we presume God would so frequently warn us of these things if the possibility of condemnation were remote or our freedom so limited that actual condemnation is rare.

The evidence leads to only one possible conclusion: we should take the Lord Jesus and His apostles who speak for Him very seriously. It is dangerous and presumptive to think they mean something other than what they plainly say. And the plain message is this: Many prefer the darkness and like their sins, dissenting opinions, and attitudes too much to really want heaven. Heaven is the antithesis of the false paradise they seek.

Through a stubborn refusal to listen to God and base our lives on what He teaches, we cannot inherit our true reward of heaven. We render ourselves incapable of enduring the bright light of God's truth and call it intolerable. Those who hate the truth see the truth as hateful and God as wrathful. At the judgment, they will be miserable and angry, but God isn't the answer they seek. As such, heaven is no place for them, and God will not force it on them. They have made their bed in hell, and God consigns them to it.

Beware, many (not few) are following this path, and if they do not repent, things will not end well. In the next chapter, we will consider some of the spiritual, psychological, and sociological reasons why hell exists and why the Lord insisted that "many" are on the wide road that leads there.

CHAPTER 4

Why Are Many on the Road to Destruction but Few to Salvation?

A Consideration of the Deep Drives of Sin in Us

The heart is deceitful above all things,
and desperately corrupt;
who can understand it?
"I the Lord search the mind
and try the heart,
to give every man according to his ways,
according to the fruit of his doings."

—Jeremiah 17:9–10

Having considered the warnings and admonitions of Jesus regarding hell and judgment, we ought next to consider some of the psychological and cultural justifications for His teaching. For, indeed, an obvious question to ask is why so many walk the wide road to spiritual destruction and why so "few" (not most) find salvation. Is it because God is stingy with graces or strict and cruel in His judgments? No. God *wants* to save us all. Scripture says, "As surely as I live, declares the Lord GOD, I take no pleasure in the

death of the wicked, but rather that the wicked should turn
from their ways and live. Turn! Turn from your evil ways!
For why should you die, O house of Israel?" (Ez 33:11).
And again, "God our Savior . . . wants everyone to be saved
and to come to the knowledge of the truth" (1 Tm 2:4). But
another aspect of God's will is that He has made us free and
we possess the power of choice. Of this, God says, "I have
set before you life and death, blessing and curse. Therefore,
choose life, that you and your offspring may live, loving the
LORD your God, obeying his voice, and holding fast to
him" (Dt 30:19–20). Yes, God respects our freedom.

So the real answer as to why there is a hell and why many
go there is that we are *hard* to save, and we must become
more sober about that. We have hard hearts, thick skulls,
and innumerable other traits that make us a difficult case.

If, as tradition holds, a third of the angels fell (cf. Rv
12:9), that ought to make us very aware of our own similar
tendency to do so and make us humbler about our own
spiritual condition. The fallen angels had intellects vastly
superior to ours, and their angelic souls were not weighed
down with the many bodily passions that beset us—but
still, they fell!

Adam and Eve, possessing preternatural gifts and exist-
ing before all the weaknesses we inherited from sin, also
fell. Are we, who are more vulnerable to temptation, really
going to claim that we are not in any real danger or that we
are easy to save? No, they who are better than us also fell
in great numbers.

We need to sober up and run to God with greater humility, admitting that we are a hard case and in desperate need

of the medicines and graces that God offers. He offers us His Word, the sacraments, holy fellowship, and lots of prayer! We need not panic, but we do need to be far more conscientious than most people are about ourselves and those we love.

Consider some of the following reasons why many are lost because they resist the admonitions of Jesus.

We Have Concupiscence

Prior to the effects of original sin, it is taught (e.g., Council of Trent, Denzinger 3514, 1926) that Adam and Eve had the preternatural gift of "integrity." That is, their human appetites and desires were completely submitted to the intellect. They had authority over passions, feelings, and desires. This is why their sin in the garden is so puzzling and serious. After the Fall ushered in original sin, things were turned upside down. The passions became unruly and demanded unreasonable attention and fulfillment. This state of excessive and irrational desires is called concupiscence. In effect, we are besieged with desires of the lower appetite contrary to reason. Because of original and personal sin, the subordination of our reason to God is damaged, and we begin to lose our sense of the supreme good and our ultimate end. If we do not discipline ourselves, the lower appetites become increasingly unrestrained, and we permit them to take control. This leads, as we can see often in ourselves and in the wider culture, to the pursuit of sensuous gratifications independent of what is reasonable. Our higher faculties become subordinated to the drives of our lower nature. We become prone to a kind of "emotional reasoning" and true reason fades away. Concupiscence pressures the will to consent and, by increasing degrees, hinders reason from considering the lawfulness or unlawfulness of moral acts. However, this does not mean that human reason and will are wholly damaged or unable to resist such desires, even though its freedom and dominion are to some extent diminished. In fact, through grace and the practice of virtue, our will can resist temptation, while vices can be mastered. Though it is a battle, the Lord mercifully offers His law, teaching, and sufficient graces to us so that, as Scripture says, where sin abounds, grace abounds all the more (see Rom 5:20; 2 Cor 12:9).

Our "Flesh" Is Opposed to Our Spirit

In every human being, there exists a spiritual nature that is open to goodness, beauty, and truth; it is a part of us that seeks God and the highest things associated with Him. But opposed to this is another deep drive that St. Paul calls "the flesh" (*sarx*, in Greek). The flesh is not to be understood simply as the body. More accurately, it is an attitude of rebellion and a deep preference for the lower things of this earth, such as wealth, power, popularity, and, yes, the inordinate desires of the body. The flesh does not want to be told what to do; it rebels against limits and thus opposes the teachings of God and His Church. Heaven and spiritual things are a bore to the flesh; its preoccupation is with worldly and trendy things, anything but God and the things of God. St. Thomas Aquinas mentions this slothful attitude of the flesh in the *Summa* and concludes, on account of it: "Those who are saved are in the minority." (Pars Prima Q. 23.7 ad 3). The flesh indulges pride and resists what is reasonable and true. St. Paul identified the bad fruits of the flesh explicitly: "Now the works of the flesh are evident: sexual immorality, impurity, sensuality, idolatry, sorcery, enmity, strife, jealousy, fits of anger, rivalries, dissensions, divisions, envy, drunkenness, orgies, and things like these" (Gal 5:19–21).

There is no time here to develop every wicked manifestation except to note that the "flesh" is a very deep drive where a lot of sinful attitudes and vices park. It is where concupiscence parks and where pride, greed, lust, anger, gluttony, envy, and sloth find a home. Christians are called upon to resist and fight sins of the flesh. Our fallen nature offers no excuse. With God's grace and the Holy Spirit interacting with our human spirit, it is a battle we can progressively win. Here again, St. Paul teaches:

> Walk by the Spirit, and you will not gratify the desires of the flesh. For the flesh craves what is contrary to the Spirit, and the Spirit what is contrary to the flesh. They are opposed to each other, so that you do not do what you want. But if you are led by the Spirit, you are not under the law. . . . Those who belong to Christ Jesus have crucified the flesh with its passions and desires. Since we live by the Spirit, let us walk in step with the Spirit. Let us not become conceited, provoking and envying one another. (Gal 5:17–18, 24–26)

There is an old saying, "If you find a good fight, get in it." And this is a good fight: the battle against concupiscence and the flesh. It can be increasingly won by the power of the cross to put sin to death. But sadly, for many, this battle is undesirable. They prefer the passing pleasure of this world to the eternal joy of heaven. They realize the battle might involve giving up some of their favorite sins. Slothful, lukewarm, distracted, and indifferent, they resist any call to battle and prefer to settle with sin. Resisting the current is too much trouble; they prefer to float downstream. And this widespread attitude explains some of the reasons why many are lost and fewer are saved. Many simply prefer the darkness.

So now let us look at the offshoots of concupiscence and the flesh if they are not resisted.

We Have Hard Hearts and Stubborn Wills

Surely these flow from the flesh and from concupiscence. But it deserves to be highlighted as a very common disposition in the human family. God, speaking to us through Isaiah the prophet, said, "I know that you are obstinate, and your neck is an iron sinew and your forehead is bronze" (Is 48:4). Note, he is talking about us and how easily defiant we can be!

We Are Obtuse in Our Desires

As an offshoot of concupiscence, we can easily note that if something is forbidden, we seem to want it all the more. Strangely, we know things that are harmful to us, but we want them in abundance. We also know things that are good for us, but we are often averse to it. We like our sweets and our salty snacks, but vegetables rot in the refrigerator. In fact, it even seems that we become averse to things *because* they are good for us! And we desire things all the more *because* they are forbidden! St. Paul laconically observed, "When the commandment came, sin sprang to life" (Rom 7:9). In the desert, the people of Israel longed for melons, leeks, onions, and the fleshpots they enjoyed in Egypt. Never mind that they were slaves then. When it came to the bread from heaven, the holy manna, they said, "We are disgusted with this wretched manna" (Nm 21:5).

So, we are obtuse. We are turned toward sin and the world rather than toward God and His holy embrace. Here again, Jesus's words about the nature of the judgment we face and why many are lost ring true: many prefer the darkness to the light of the kingdom (Jn 3:19).

We Don't Like to Be Told What to Do

We bristle at correction. Even if we know a correction is needed and true, that we ought to do something or to stop doing something, the mere fact that someone is telling us often makes us dig in our heels and refuse. And if we comply, we often do so resentfully rather than wholeheartedly.

We Are Not Docile

To be docile means to be teachable. When we were very young, we were fascinated with the world around us and kept asking, "Why, Mommy?" or "Why, Daddy?" As we got older, our skull thickened. We stopped asking why. We figured we knew better than anyone around us. The problem just worsens with age unless grace intervenes. St. Paul lamented, "For the time will come when people will not endure sound doctrine; but wanting to have their ears tickled, they will accumulate for themselves teachers in accordance to their own desires, and will turn away their ears from the truth and will turn aside to myths" (2 Tm 4:3–5).

We Love Distraction and Don't Listen

Even when saving knowledge is offered to us, we are too often tuned out, distracted, and unwilling to hear it. Attention deficit disorder is nothing new in the human family. God said through Jeremiah, "To whom shall I speak and give warning, that they may hear? Behold, their ears are uncircumcised, they cannot listen; behold, the word of the LORD is to them an object of scorn; they take no pleasure in it" (Jer 6:10). Note that this text speaks not only of distraction but of a willful distraction. We are often distracted because we want to be distracted. Sitting quietly and listening carefully to the Lord is, in some sense, terrifying. So, instead, we seek out YouTube videos or lose ourselves in social media. Jesus invoked Isaiah to explain why He spoke to the crowds only in parables: "For this people's heart has grown dull, and with their ears they can barely hear, and their eyes they have closed" (Is 6:10).

We Are Opinionated

We tend to think that something is true or right merely because we think it or agree with it. There is a saying: "Don't believe everything you think." We usually smile when hearing this because we know just how deep that tendency is.

Most of our views and opinions are stubbornly and pridefully held. We cannot bother with facts when our mind is made up. There is nothing wrong with having opinions, even strong ones, when it is about what is certainly right and true. But it is amazing how often we stubbornly resist even when Scripture or the Church's formal teaching challenges our opinion. Never mind that God is just a little smarter than we are. His official teaching in the Scripture and the Doctrine of the Church is inspired; our opinions are not. Scripture says of our human tendency to be opinionated, "All we, like sheep, have gone astray, each of us has turned to our own way" (Is 53:6). Or again, "Can the pot say to the potter, 'You know nothing'?" (Is 29:16). And yet again, "Woe to those who quarrel with their Maker, those who are nothing but potsherds among the potsherds on the ground. Does the clay say to the potter, 'What are you making?'" (Is 45:9). Despite this, many go on with their own opinions and will not abide even the clear correction of God. This leads to a refusal to repent and a defiance that can land one in hell.

We Have Darkened Intellects Due to Unruly and Dominating Passions

Our strong and unruly passions cloud our mind and seek to compel our will. As we saw above, without training and practice in virtue, our baser faculties come to dominate our higher faculties, making unreasonable demands for satisfaction. We love to tell ourselves lots of lies. We suppress the truth and our senseless minds become darkened (cf. Rom 1:21). The

Catechism says, "The human mind . . . is hampered in the attaining of . . . truths, not only by the impact of the senses and the imagination, but also by disordered appetites which are the consequences of original sin. So it happens that men in such matters easily persuade themselves that what they would not like to be true is false or at least doubtful" (*CCC* 37; quoting from Pius XII's work *Humani Generis*, 561: DS 3875).

The Second Vatican Council, in *Lumen Gentium* 16, says, "But often men, deceived by the Evil One, have become vain in their reasonings and have exchanged the truth of God for a lie, serving the creature rather than the Creator."

We Are Lemmings

We are too easily swayed by what is popular. We prefer modern notions to ancient and tested wisdom. Whatever the fad or fashion, no matter how foolish, harmful, or immodest, many clamor for it. Hollywood stars get divorces, and soon enough, everyone is casting aside biblical teaching against it. The same goes for many other moral issues. What was once thought disgraceful is now celebrated and paraded on Main Street. Like lemmings, we run along with the crowd to celebrate what was once called sin (and is *still* sinful). Instead of following God, we follow human beings. We follow them and the "culture" they create, often mindlessly.

We Live in a Fallen World with Fallen Natures Governed by a Fallen Angel

Many seem to abide by all of this quite well. We will so easily make compromises to build our place in this world.

Rare today is the longing for heaven or a sober appreciation of the Lord's warnings about wealth and worldliness. Even our so-called spiritual life is mainly predominated by prayers for the Lord to improve our worldly standing. So not only is the fear of hell largely diminished today, so is the longing for heaven. Few sermons, seminars, or retreats make much mention of heaven, let alone focus on it. You'd almost never know that the one and only goal of our whole existence is to be with God forever in heaven, in joys unspeakable and glories untold. If heaven is mentioned, it is usually at funerals but in a rather presumptuous and sentimental way that does not inspire the necessary repentance and the battle along the narrow way to get there.

Honorable Mention

Hence there are many psychological, spiritual, and sociological reasons that hell is a destination of many, not few. And if all the above isn't enough, consider a few other drives and attitudes that are often not repented of and which are of the wide road that leads to destruction. We are so often obnoxious, dishonest, egotistical, undisciplined, weak, impure, arrogant, self-centered, pompous, insincere, unchaste, grasping, harsh, impatient, shallow, inconsistent, unfaithful, immoral, ungrateful, disobedient, selfish, lukewarm, slothful, unloving, uncommitted, untrusting, indifferent, hateful, lazy, cowardly, angry, greedy, jealous, vengeful, prideful, envious, contemptuous, stingy, petty, spiteful, indulgent, careless, neglectful, prejudiced, and just plain mean.

And, as St. Louis Marie De Monfort has memorably observed, "By nature, we are prouder than peacocks, more groveling than toads, more vile than unclean animals, more envious than serpents, more gluttonous than hogs, more furious than tigers, lazier than tortoises, weaker than reeds, and more capricious than weathercocks. We have within ourselves nothing but nothingness and sin, and we deserve nothing but the anger of God and everlasting hell" (*True Devotion*, no. 79).

Do you still think hell is largely empty? There are many reasons, some of which are presented here, that show a widespread resistance to the grace and mercy of God. In some cases, it is a lukewarm disinterestedness in what God offers. But in other cases, it is an even more troubling stubbornness, even defiance, to what God teaches and offers. And none of the things detailed here are all that subtle or rare.

Summary

So, if the road to destruction is wide (as Jesus said), don't blame God. The road is wide for reasons like these. We are a hard case; we are hard to save. It is not that God lacks power; it is that we refuse to overcome many of these shortcomings. God, who made us free, will not force us to change.

We ought not to kid ourselves into thinking that we can go on defying the kingdom of God and its values, yet magically, at death, we will suddenly want to enter His kingdom, which we have resisted our whole lives. However, many *prefer* the darkness. Is it likely that their preference will suddenly shift? Will not the glorious light of heaven seem harsh, blinding, and even repulsive to them? In such a case, is not God's "Depart from me" both a just and merciful response? Why force a person who hates the light to live in it? I suppose it grieves God to have to witness such a departure, but to force a person to endure Him would be even more difficult. I am sure it is with great sadness that God accepts a person's final no.

Hence, the road is wide that leads to destruction, and it is wide because of *us*. The narrow road is the way of the cross, which is a stumbling block and an absurdity to many (cf. 1 Cor 1:23), who simply will not abide its message.

A proper response is that we ought to be sober about the Lord's lament. We ought also to be more urgent in our attempts to subdue our own unruly soul and the souls of those we love for the kingdom. The blasé attitude of most moderns is rooted in the extremely flawed notion that judgment and hell are not real. That is a lie, for it contradicts Jesus's clear word.

We ought not to be unduly fearful or panicked, but we ought to run to Jesus in humility and beg Him to save us from our worst enemy—our very self. If you don't think you're a hard case, read the paragraph of vices listed above and think again.

CHAPTER 5

What Is the Wrath of God?

Does Hell Exist Because God Is Angry?

"For God did not appoint us to suffer wrath but to receive salvation through our Lord Jesus Christ."

—1 Thessalonians 5:9

"But because of your stubbornness and your unrepentant heart, you are storing up wrath against yourself for the day of God's wrath, when his righteous judgment will be revealed."

—Romans 2:5

The drama of judgment, the need for repentance, and the reality of hell is a constant theme of Jesus's preaching. Many prefer the wide road to destruction because they fail to accept God's graces to take up the battle against our lower, fleshly nature and resist God's invitation to heal the concupiscence that came from original sin. In the last chapter, many sources and reasons for this resistance were identified. However, explanations are not merely excuses. The Lord teaches us to engage the battle that life in this world entails and His grace will be sufficient for each one of us. Failing in this effort amounts to resistance to the warnings and teachings of the prophetic Word of God in Scripture, Sacred Tradition, and the natural law of the "book" of creation. To whatever degree a person's freedom was hindered by matters beyond his control, God, who is just, will surely take such cases into account. However, because these challenges are exceptions, our intellect and free will gifted to us by God come with responsibility about which we must be sober and serious.

We now return to another objection—namely, that hell presents an image of an angry God that many reject. Indeed, many today trivialize God, thinking of Him more as the great affirmer or a doting grandfather. Jesus, too, has been reduced to merely a healer and a kind of harmless hippie. These caricatures must be corrected by Scripture itself. God does love us and is the great healer. But He also expects to be taken seriously and is not about to reduce healing to whatever we want it to mean. He loves us too much for that and will not lie to us. True healing will include suffering as well as consolation. Only the truth can really set us free. God is not angry, but He, like any good doctor, will not fail to summon us to lifestyle changes and call, at times, for strong medicine, including painful surgeries. But there is another aspect of God's "anger" that must be explored. For Scripture does speak of God's "wrath" quite frequently. In this chapter, we examine this biblical theme and seek to understand it more deeply so that we do not perpetuate another caricature of God—namely, as One who is angry and moody. The teaching about God's wrath can be subtle and may lead us to unexpected places.

So, as noted, God's wrath is spoken of often in Scripture. It is not merely an Old Testament concept but occurs frequently in the New Testament. Consider just a few examples.

- "Jesus said, 'Whoever believes in the Son has eternal life, but whoever rejects the Son will not see life, for God's wrath remains upon him'" (Jn 3:36).
- "Do not take revenge, my friends, but leave room for God's wrath, for it is written: 'It is mine to avenge; I will repay,' says the Lord" (Rom 12:19).
- "Let no one deceive you with empty words, for because of such things [e.g., sexual immorality] God's wrath comes on those who are disobedient" (Eph 5:6).
- "For God did not appoint us to suffer wrath but to receive salvation through our Lord Jesus Christ" (1 Thes 5:9).
- "The angel swung his sickle on the earth, gathered its grapes and threw them into the great winepress of God's wrath" (Rv 14:19).

Clearly, the "wrath of God" is not some ancient or primitive concept with which the New Testament dispensed. Notice also that the wrath of God is not something reserved for the end of the world; it is spoken of as already operative in certain people.

However, the wrath of God concept must be treated with due care. There are some today who simply dismiss the concept as contrary to God's love. But that is to deny many Scriptures which do attribute wrath to the God of Love. But it is also wrong and simplistic to understand the wrath of God as merely meaning that God is angry or in some sort of bad mood. God is not moody. He is not subject to passions as we are, and He does not change. Scripture says of Him:

- "He is the Father of lights, with whom is no variableness, neither shadow of turning" (Jas 1:17).
- "I, the LORD, do not change" (Mal 3:6).
- "You remain the same O Lord, and Your years will never end" (Ps 102:27).
- "Lord, you will roll up the heavens like a robe; like a garment they will be changed; but You remain the same" (Heb 1:12).
- "Jesus Christ is the same yesterday and today and forever" (Heb 13:8).

So, God is not moody. He is not beset by fits of anger and rage interspersed with arbitrary moments of mercy and patience.

All this just intensifies our curiosity and compels us to ask, "What is the wrath of God?"

Simply put, God's wrath is our experience of the total incompatibility of our sinful state before the holiness of God. Sin and God's holiness just don't mix; they can't keep company. Think of fire and water; they cannot coexist in the same place. Bring them together and you can hear the conflict. Think of water spilled on a hot stovetop: the water droplets sizzle and pop; steam rises as the water boils away. If there is a lot of water in the presence of fire, the fire is overwhelmed and extinguished. When water and fire meet, conflict ensues, and only one will win. This is God's wrath: the complete incompatibility of two things—our unrequited sin and God's utter holiness. We must purify ourselves before entering His presence; otherwise, we cannot tolerate the intensity of His glory. We would wail and grind our teeth, turning away in horror. The wrath is the conflict between our sin and God's holiness. God cannot and will not change, so we must change, or else we will experience wrath.

To illustrate further, consider the following analogy: On the ceiling of a bedroom is a light fixture with a 100-watt bulb. Before bed at night, we delight in the light and are accustomed to it. At bedtime, we turn off the light and go to sleep. If we wake up in the middle of the night and turn on the same light, what happens? We squint to protect our eyes from the harsh bright light. Obviously, the light itself has not changed; it is just as bright in the early morning hours as it was the previous evening. The light is the same, but *we* have changed. The light is not any harsher than it was the night before when we were perfectly happy with it. Now that we have changed, we experience its "wrath," but the wrath is really in us.

Consider an example from the Old Testament. Adam and Eve walked with God in the cool of the evening when the dew collected on the grass (*see* Gn 3:8). They had a warm friendship with Him and did not fear His presence. But after sinning, they hid in fear of Him. Did God change? No, *they* changed. They now experienced Him very differently. Next, let us fast forward to another theophany. God had come to

Mt. Sinai, and as He descended, the people were terrified, for there were peals of thunder, lightning, clouds, and the blast of a trumpet. The people told Moses, *"You speak to us, and we will listen, but let not God speak to us, else we will die"* (Ex 20:19). God, too, warned Moses that the people could not get close lest His wrath be vented upon them (Ex 19:20–25). Had God changed? No, He was the same God who had walked with Adam and Eve in the cool of the evening in a most intimate way. We were the ones who changed. We had lost the holiness without which no one can see the Lord (Heb 12:14). The same God, unchanged though He was, now seemed frightening and wrathful.

And so, the primary location of God's wrath is not in Him; it is in us. God does not change; He is holy and serene; He is love. We are to blame if we experience His wrath. It is we who change, not God.

To the degree that "wrath" is within God Himself, it is not a volatile passion that flares up from time to time in the form of a tantrum. It is, rather, a stable disposition that sets itself against injustice and sin, and what that does to the people He loves. God's wrath is His "passion" to set things right. And to a large degree, we expect this from Him. We trust that those who have harmed us or others we love will answer to God for what they have done. Simply overlooking every sin and crime offends against justice and, frankly, isn't merciful either. Part of God's justice, as well as His mercy, is that He requites victims of injustice and crime by having offenders render an account for what they have done. God's mercy seeks to set things right and to reestablish justice in the face of injustice.

God also permits His holiness to be experienced by us as wrath for our own personal growth in holiness. He further promises to get us ready for our encounter with Him at our judgment so that, as Scripture says, we may joyfully and properly "await His Son from heaven, whom He raised from the dead—Jesus who delivers us from the coming wrath" (1 Thes 1:10).

If we can allow the image of fire to remain before us, we may well find a hopeful sign in God's providence. If God is a holy fire, a consuming fire (cf. Heb 12:26; Is 33:14), how can we possibly come into His presence? How can we avoid the wrath that would destroy us? Well, what is the only thing that survives in the presence of fire? Fire! It looks as if we'd better *become* fire if we want to see God. He sent tongues of fire upon the apostles and upon us at our Confirmation. God wants us to become holy by setting us on fire with the Holy Spirit. He wants to ignite a spiritual fire in us so that we can stand in His presence. "Behold, I send my messenger to prepare the way before me, and the Lord whom you seek will suddenly come to his temple; the messenger of the covenant in whom you delight, behold, he is coming, says the Lord of hosts. But who can endure the day of his coming, and who can stand when he appears? For he is like a refiner's fire and like fullers' soap; he will sit as a refiner and purifier of silver, and he will purify the sons of Levi and refine them like gold and silver" (Mal 3:1–3).

And if the Lord does this and we cooperate with Him, we can endure the day of His coming. Of that day, the Lord says there will be two experiences of the same reality:

For behold, the day comes, burning like an oven, when all the arrogant and all evildoers will be stubble; the day that comes shall burn them up, says the Lord of hosts, so that it will leave them neither root nor branch. But for you who fear my name the sun of righteousness shall rise, with healing in its wings. You shall go forth leaping like calves from the stall. And you shall tread down the wicked, for they will be ashes under the soles of your feet, on the day when I act, says the Lord of hosts. (Mal 4:1–3)

Two groups will experience the fiery day of judgment in two very different ways. The first group, the unrepentant evildoers, will experience a blazing wrath, the total incompatibility of their sinful state before the holiness of God. For the second group, those who fear the Lord's name, the weather will seem perfect, for God's fiery love will seem like the gentle and healing rays of the rising sun at dawn. God is not personally wrathful to one group and gentle toward another. He is always the same and one reality. Your experience of judgment will depend ultimately on the group to which you belong.

So, what will it be for us on judgment day? Blazing wrath or healing rays? You decide. Fortunately, now that Jesus has come, there is a way for us to enter God's presence without wrath. Scripture says: "For you have turned to God from idols to serve the living and true God, and to wait for his Son from heaven, whom he raised from the dead—Jesus, who rescues us from the coming wrath" (1 Thes 1:10–11).

So, There Is a "Wrath Of God," and It Is More in Us Than It Is in Him

Wrath is *our* experience of the incompatibility of sin before God. We must be washed clean in the Blood of the Lamb and purified. Most of us will need purification in purgatory, too. However, if we let the Lord perform His saving work, we will be saved from the wrath, for we are made holy and set on fire with His love—and fire doesn't fear the presence of fire. God is love, but He will not change; His love must change us.

CHAPTER 6

Why Is Hell Eternal?

Is There No Repentance in Hell?

"And they will go away into eternal punishment,
but the righteous into eternal life."

—Matthew 25:46

Now that we have been able to conclude that hell exists because of God's respect for our freedom and not because He is merely mad or unforgiving, the following question remains to be answered: Why is hell eternal? Why should we be punished eternally for finite crimes? Are not the souls in hell sorry for what they have done? Does God refuse to hear their penitent cries? Why does Jesus say they go off to eternal punishment (cf. Mt 25:46) where there is eternal fire and "their worm does not die" (see Mk 9:48)? It all seems cruel to the modern mind.

Here we encounter a mystery about ourselves. God seems to be teaching us that there will come a day when our decisions are fixed forever. Therefore, if hell is eternal, it is not because God refuses ever to forgive but because our decision to turn from His kingdom and its values is forever fixed. In this world, we always have the opportunity to change our mind, so the idea of a permanent decision seems strange to us. However, those of us who are older can testify that, as we age, we get more set in our ways; it's harder and harder to change. Perhaps this is a little foretaste of a time when our decisions will be forever fixed, and we will never change. The Fathers of the Church used an image of pottery to teach this lesson. Think of wet clay on a potter's wheel. If the clay is moist and still on the wheel, it can be shaped and reshaped, but once it is put in the kiln, in the fire, its shape is fixed forever. So it is with us that when we appear before God, who is a holy fire, our fundamental shape will be forever fixed, our decisions will be final. This is mysterious to us, and we only sense it vaguely, but because heaven and hell are eternal, it seems reasonable to conclude that this forever-fixed state is in our future.

To further illustrate this fixity of our decision, consider the well-known story of Lazarus and the rich man. On one level, the message of the story seems plain enough: neglecting the poor is a damnable sin. However, there are other important teachings about death, judgment, heaven, and hell. Those teachings are hidden in the details, but the subtlety is part of the story's beauty. Let's look at some of the teachings, beginning with the obvious one.

In the first place, as noted, neglect of the poor is a damnable sin. The vision of Lazarus's poverty is dramatic indeed. He sits at the rich man's gate, hungry and alone, while the rich man dines sumptuously. Dogs lick the sores of Lazarus. The unnamed rich man (dubbed Dives by some because it means "rich" in Latin) does not so much as act in an evil way toward Lazarus. He does not beat, curse, or directly abuse him. Rather, he commits the sin of neglect and omission. He seems undisturbed by and removed from Lazarus's suffering. This neglect, this insensitivity, lands him in hell. The text says, "The rich man died and was buried, and from the netherworld, where he was in torment, he raised his eyes." Care for the poor will be a central theme of our judgment, as is made clear in the Gospel of Matthew (25:31 ff), in which Jesus separates the sheep from the goats, the just from the unrighteous, based on whether they cared for the least of their brethren. To those who neglected the poor, the Lord Jesus says, "Depart from me, you who are cursed, into the eternal fire prepared for the devil and his angels" (Mt 25:41).

How best to care for the poor is a matter of some dispute, but the fact that we must care for them is undeniable. Hence, the rich man who neglected Lazarus is now in hell.

But secondly, notice a more subtle point. Although Dives is in torment, he has not changed. The text says of him, "The rich man, in torment, raised his eyes and saw Abraham far off and Lazarus at his side. And he cried out, 'Father Abraham, have pity on me. Send Lazarus to dip the tip of his finger in water and cool my tongue, for I am suffering torment in these flames.'"

Notice that the rich man still fails to see Lazarus's dignity. In effect, he still sees Lazarus as of little significance. And though he has to look up to see him, the rich man still looks down on Lazarus. He does not ask Abraham to send Lazarus to him so that he can apologize for his sinful neglect and seek his forgiveness. Rather, he merely wants Lazarus to serve him. Even though he is in torment, the rich man is unrepentant. Although he doesn't like where he is, Dives does not reconcile with Lazarus or even seem to accept that he should do so. This rich man is hardened in his sin. While Lazarus was alive, the rich man never recognized his dignity, and now in death, he remains blind to it.

And so, for us, sin hardens our heart over time. The more we remain in sin, the harder our hearts become and the less likely it is that we will ever change. And thus, we learn that Dives cannot and will not change; his decision, character, and demeanor are forever fixed.

There is an old litany that goes like this:

> Sow a thought, reap a deed;
> sow a deed, reap a habit;
> sow a habit, reap a character;
> sow a character, reap a destiny.

The mystery of the world to come is that our character is forever fixed. St. Paul teaches that God will judge as through fire (see 1 Cor 3:12–15). Like the clay taken from the potter's wheel and brought to the kiln, the judgment through fire will either purify us or bring us condemnation. The fixed quality of the human person is illustrated in the rich man's unchanged attitude. It is this way for us when we come before God.

Thirdly, notice the strangest thing of all. The rich man does not ask that he might come to heaven; rather, he asks that Lazarus be sent to hell! One of the saddest facts about the souls in hell is that they would not be happy in heaven anyway. After all, heaven is about being with God. It is about justice, love of the poor, chastity, the heavenly liturgy, the celebration of the truth, the praise of God. God is at the center rather than us. As already noted, many show by the way they live that they do not want many of these godly things. Why would someone who has disliked, even hated, the things of God suddenly become enamored of them at the moment of death? Someone who ignores or disdains God and considers His faithful to be hypocrites would hardly be happy in heaven.

The rich man demonstrates this by the fact that he does not ask to come to heaven. He surely does not like where he is, but he shows no repentant desire for heaven either. In truth, he can't ask to come to heaven since his disposition against it and its values is forever fixed. The teaching, though subtle, seems clear enough: the souls in hell have little interest in heaven despite their dislike of Satan's torments.

A fourth truth is also represented in this parable, that of the great reversal. Abraham says to Dives, "My child, remember that you received what was good during your lifetime while Lazarus likewise received what was bad; but now he is comforted here, whereas you are tormented."

We spend a lot of time trying to be on top in this world. We want comfort, wealth, position, and power. Here, the Lord warns us of the coming great reversal. Lazarus, who was poor, is now rich, while the rich man is now poor.

Jesus teaches this elsewhere: "But many who are first will be last, and the last first" (Mk 10:31). The Virgin Mother Mary proclaimed how God has reversed many things: "He has brought down the mighty from their thrones and lifted up the humble. He has filled the hungry with good things but has sent the rich away empty" (Lk 1:51–53).

This is a great reversal. We so want to be rich and comfortable in this world, running from any suffering or setback. But the Lord warns of riches: "How hard it is for the rich to enter the kingdom of God" (Mk 10:23). Yet still, we want to be rich. He also says, "Anyone who does not carry his cross and follow me cannot be my disciple" (Lk 14:27). Yet we run from the cross and suffering. In the great reversal, many who are first in this world will be last in the world to come.

We cannot assert a direct correlation between success here and loss in the world to come, but neither should we ignore the teaching that striving to "make it" in the world and "be somebody" can be a dangerous path. And if we have amounted to something, we'd better humble ourselves through generosity to the poor and associating with the humble. The goal of worldly success is a dangerous one, for the great reversal is coming. Better to be found among the humble and the poor, or at least well-associated with them, than to be mighty and high. Yes, beware of the great reversal!

And finally, we are taught in this parable that it is a bad idea to feign ignorance of our moral duties. Refusing the truth of Revelation is a damnable sin. The rich man, while alive, did not heed God's Word or repent of his omissions. Even now he does not seek to be reconciled with Lazarus or express sorrow for what he failed to do. But he does have some concerns for his brothers, for his family who are still living in the world and can change. We need not assume that the souls in hell have no affections whatsoever. However, their affections are not for God and what He esteems. And so, the rich man, still viewing Lazarus only as an errand boy, asks Abraham to dispatch Lazarus to his family carrying a warning. Perhaps a vision from the grave will convince them!

But Abraham indicates quite clearly that they have the clear witness of God through Moses and the prophets. In other words, they have the Scriptures, the very Word of God, to warn them. The rich man insists, "Oh no, father Abraham, but if someone from the dead goes to them, they will repent." Then Abraham said, "If they will not listen to Moses and the prophets, neither will they be persuaded if someone should rise from the dead."

The last point is dripping with irony because Jesus would rise from the dead. Abraham says clearly that there are many sinners who are so hardened in their sin that no matter what the Scriptures say, the natural law sets forth, or the Church solemnly teaches, they will never be convinced. Nothing has changed since then. No amount of Scripture or Church teaching will convince them that they are wrong. This is what happens to us if we remain in unrepented sin: our hearts are hardened, our minds are closed, and our necks are stiffened. In the end, Jesus's parable teaches that such hardness grows and that after death, the hardness and refusal to repent becomes permanent. While the passage does strongly imply that Dives's punishment is deserved, why should his penalty be eternal? Therefore, it also seems implied that a chasm exists that cannot be crossed even if one wanted to. Thus, something is no longer available either to Lazarus or Dives. It is proposed here that the "chasm" is the inability to alter one's fundamental acceptance of, or rejection of God and His kingdom. Hell is eternal not because God is unforgiving or vengeful. Hell is forever because of our "no" to

God and His heavenly kingdom. In brief, we cannot repent after death since our character is now quickened and our choice is forever fixed.

St. Thomas Aquinas addresses the question of whether the souls in hell can or do repent. While concluding that, after death, repentance in the formal sense is not possible, he makes an important distinction. He teaches, "A person may repent of sin in two ways: in one way directly, in another way indirectly. He repents of a sin directly who hates sin as such: and he repents indirectly who hates it on account of something connected with it, for instance punishment or something of that kind. Accordingly, the wicked will not repent of their sins directly, because consent in the malice of sin will remain in them; but they will repent indirectly, inasmuch as they will suffer from the punishment inflicted on them for sin" (*Summa Theologica*, Supplement, q. 98, art. 2).

This explains the "wailing and grinding of teeth" insofar as it points to the lament of the damned. They do not lament their choice to sin, but they do lament the consequences. Just because they do not like where they are, it does not follow that they desire heaven just as it is. They want relief from their misery and frustration, but on their terms, not God's. Thus, in the parable of Lazarus, the rich man in hell laments his suffering but expresses no regret over the way he treated the beggar, Lazarus. His defiant and insensitive sinfulness is fixed and unchangeable.

And thus, we return to the opening question of this chapter and let St. Thomas have the last word. Is eternal punishment just? Why should one be punished eternally for sins committed over a brief time span, perhaps in just a moment?

The punishment does not seem to fit the crime. This logic presumes that the eternal nature of hell is intrinsic to the punishment, but it is not. Rather, as noted, hell is eternal not as a punishment from God per se but because repentance is no longer available after death.

St. Thomas teaches, "As Damascene says (*De Fide Orth.* ii) 'death is to men what their fall was to the angels.' Now after their fall the angels could not be restored [cf. S.T. I:64:2]. Therefore, neither can man after death: and thus the punishment of the damned will have no end. . . . [So] just as the demons are obstinate in wickedness and therefore have to be punished for ever, so too are the souls of men who die without charity, since 'death is to men what their fall was to the angels,' as Damascene says" (*Summa Theologica*, Supplement, q. 99, art. 3).

CHAPTER 7

What Is Hell Like?

Insights from the Lord, St. Thomas, and Others

"If you're going through hell, keep going."

—Winston Churchill

"Those who promise us paradise on earth
never produced anything but a hell."

—Karl Popper

As we ponder some images of hell in this chapter, we should note that not all of them are of equal authority. Surely the Lord's own descriptions are most authoritative. But even His descriptions are of a general nature and seem to be intentionally vivid. The visions of the saints carry weight, but Catholics are not required to put faith in their visions. A third tier of teachings is somewhat in the realm of speculation, and these come to us from theologians and some of the Church Fathers. Their speculations are not wild speculations, however. St. Thomas Aquinas applies the use of reason to known truths in answering questions that arise in our minds about hell. For example, he teaches we can rightly conclude that since God is just, not all in hell suffer in the same way. Even though Jesus does not develop such distinctions, it is reasonable to conclude this based on other truths in Scripture. Dante made a similar conclusion.

We turn first to the Lord Jesus's own teachings. Part of what makes Jesus's teaching on hell difficult is His severe imagery. When discussing hell, He seems to point to its deepest pits. He warns of eternal fire, undying worms, and wailing and grinding of teeth. Rather than lingering on philosophical explanations, Jesus goes to the deepest aspects of the sufferings of hell and what can result in the heart, mind, and body of those who persist in serious sins.

Vivid though these descriptions of hell are, it is not as though we do not see many of these aspects here on earth. Sexual sins have led to more than seventy million abortions in this nation since 1973. It is an almost unimaginable blood bath. Wars in the last century killed hundreds of millions, often in horrifying fire-bombing, carpet-bombing, and even nuclear annihilation. Still others were killed in concentration camps, others in killing fields and gulags, while millions were starved to death in places like Ukraine and China.

Indeed, the hearts of so many seethe with hatred and vengeance, often leading to murder in families and neighborhoods, burned and looted cities, and violence overflowing into war and genocide. Other sins can lead to horrifying addictions that ravage the addict and harm their loved ones to some extent. Lies and deceptions fuel cynicism; injustices spur hatred. Sexual sins cause disease, abuse, loss of innocence, sexual confusion, and even sexual trafficking and

slavery. Rampant divorce ruins families and children pay
an awful price. The diagnosis of suffering humanity is grim.
The world burns with seething anger, wrathful unforgiveness, and uncontrollable passion that debase and victimize
the human person. Only those with an excessively rosy and
unrealistic view of fallen human nature could believe that
hell is empty.

The point is that the vivid accounts of hell given by
Jesus are not so hard to imagine. The fiery consequences
of sin—hatred and vengeance represented by wailing and
grinding of teeth, the devouring worms of debauchery and
dissipation, and the outer darkness of deep confusion—
are already well-known in this world of sin. For those who
die unrepentant, who prefer the darkness to the light of
the kingdom of heaven, things will only get worse. Jesus
says, "If then the light within you is darkness, how great is
the darkness!" (Mt 6:23). It is as if to say, "If you call the
darkness 'light,' you have no idea just how deep the true
darkness will be for you."

With this in mind, we turn to Jesus's vivid descriptions of
hell. If these words seem difficult, remember that they come
from Jesus, who loves you and wants to save you. He teaches
this in love and to warn us of what we already know—
namely, that unrepented sins lead to very dark places. In
chapter 3, we considered a great number of passages where
Jesus speaks of hell and describes it. From that number, consider just these five by way of reminder:

1. "But I say to you that every one who is angry with his
    brother shall be liable to judgment; whoever insults

his brother shall be liable to the council, and whoever says, 'You fool!' shall be liable to the hell of fire" (Mt 5:22).

2. "And he called out, 'Father Abraham, have mercy upon me, and send Lazarus to dip the end of his finger in water and cool my tongue; for I am in anguish in this flame'" (Lk 16:24).

3. "Then he will say to those at his left hand, 'Depart from me, you cursed, into the eternal fire prepared for the devil and his angels; for I was hungry and you gave me no food'" (Mt 25:41–42).

4. "Then the king said to the attendants, 'Bind him hand and foot, and cast him into the outer darkness; there men will weep and gnash their teeth'" (Mt 22:13).

5. "And if your hand causes you to sin, cut it off; it is better for you to enter life maimed than with two hands to go to hell, to the unquenchable fire" (Mk 9:43–44).

Allow these to suffice. Jesus, in His description, draws rather heavily from Isaiah, wherein God says of those who are unrepentant, "And they shall go forth and look on the dead bodies of the men that have rebelled against me; for their worm shall not die, their fire shall not be quenched, and they shall be an abhorrence to all flesh" (Is 66:24).

Let's consider some of these images.

Fire That Never Dies

Central to the imagery of hell is fire, although things of lesser importance make an appearance, such as worms that never die. We do well to ponder these images carefully. For while many take them literally, they are probably meant to be understood in less material and more otherworldly terms. To be sure, most of the Fathers and tradition understand the fire of hell to be an actual, physical fire, but it remains a question as to what effect physical fire would have on fallen angels who have no physical bodies. And while fallen human souls will eventually have their bodies, it seems hard to imagine how physical fire can affect their souls prior to the resurrection of the bodies of the dead. Hence, fire and other physical descriptions most likely speak also to deeper spiritual realities as well as physical ones.

Let's look at a passage from the book of Revelation and ponder what the image is trying to teach us about the nature and reality of hell for those who choose to live there by rejecting the kingdom of God and its values.

> Then I saw a great white throne and him who sat upon it; from his presence earth and sky fled away, and no place was found for them. And I saw the dead, great and small, standing before the throne, and books were opened. Also another book was opened, which is the book of life. And the dead were judged by what was written in the books, by what they had done. And the sea gave up the dead in it, Death and Hades gave up the dead in them, and all were judged by what they had done. Then Death and Hades were thrown into

the lake of fire. This is the second death, the lake of
fire; and if any one's name was not found written in
the book of life, he was thrown into the lake of fire.
(Rv 20:11–15)

A pool of fire is a dramatic metaphor. It is so dramatic,
in fact, that it causes many moderns to reject outright the
teaching of Jesus on hell. Even many who are otherwise
believers in Jesus reject His consistent teaching on judgment
and hell by either conveniently ignoring it or by espousing
some artful theories that deny He said it or that suggest He
was just trying to scare people who lived in less "sophisti-
cated" times. Some who do not believe in God point to this
teaching to justify their lack of faith. Because these objections are partially the result of ignorance, it is necessary to
focus on what this metaphor is likely trying to teach us.

Though tradition does believe the fires of hell take a physical form, there is a deeper theological meaning below the
surface imagery. For fallen angels without bodies (and for
whom the fire was first prepared) *do* experience its pain. But
how? And for fallen human souls (at least before the resurrection of the body), how is the fire experienced and to what
does it point?

Perhaps Origen, the third-century Church Father, can
provide an answer: "Wonder not when you hear that there is
a fire which though unseen has power to torture, when you
see that there is an internal fever which comes upon men
and pains them grievously" (quoted in the *Catena Aurea* at
Mat 25:41).

And thus, we gain some insight into the "inner" fire that rages in the fallen angels and in the souls of the damned. For even now, we often speak metaphorically of how our own passions can burn like fire. We speak of burning with lust, or of seething with anger, or being furious ("fury" being related to the word for fire). We speak of the heat of passion, of boiling over with anger, or of seething with envy. Even good emotions like love can burn like fire if they are not satisfied. How our thirsts and passions can rage like fire in us if they are not slaked or satiated by the only One who can truly satisfy us!

Finally, St. Thomas adds the insight of the fire as "burning" in the sense that it limits the fallen angels and fallen souls:

> But the corporeal fire is enabled as the instrument of the vengeance of Divine justice thus to detain a spirit; and thus, it has a penal effect on it, by hindering it from fulfilling its own will, that is by hindering it from acting where it will and as it will . . . that as the instrument of Divine justice [fire] is enabled to detain [a spirit] enchained as it were, and in this respect this fire is really hurtful to the spirit, and thus the soul seeing the fire as something hurtful to it is tormented by the fire (*S. T.* Supplement, q. 70, art. 3, respondeo).

In other words, someone who is no longer able to find satisfaction by following his own will seethes with indignation. Such apparent satisfaction is a lie, for it is rooted in the willful rejection of God and the values of His kingdom. The fire is a limiting fire that attests to the fact that nothing outside

God will satisfy, and that roaming about seeking satisfaction in anything other than God must now end. The fire burns and is unquenchable, for only God can quench it. But the fallen souls and fallen angels have forever refused Him.

Worms That Do Not Die

To fire, Jesus also adds the image of worms that die not. We often speak of being devoured by our passions or consumed by them. There is less consensus on the worms being physical, but surely here, too, physical or not, they speak to a deeper spiritual reality. The worms, real and allegorical, gnaw at and devour what little energy the rage has not already burned away. Unjust anger is ultimately exhausting; it saps life the way worms do. Their gnawing brings weariness and weakness, lethargy and listlessness. Depression is anger turned inward. Anger saps us in the same way intestinal worms weaken the physical body.

So, the burning fire and devouring worms of hell speak also to deeper spiritual struggles. We were made for God, and God alone can satisfy us. To choose anything less than God is to remain gravely unfulfilled. Thus, one burns with desire but has rejected the "one thing necessary" to satisfy that desire. The fire seethes, and the fury grows.

And thus, the fire of passion forever burns unsatisfied in the damned and, like worms, their desires devour and consume them. In a word, hell is the state of being "unfulfilled" forever; it is a "place" where unrepentant sinners burn with a never-ending desire because the only source of satisfaction has been rejected.

Wailing and Grinding of Teeth

As for the wailing and grinding of teeth, this double image makes it clear that it has nothing to do with sorrowful repentance. The wailing is linked to anger, expressed in the grinding of teeth. This is an angry sorrow at having been conquered or bested, the reaction of a resentful loser. The defiant refusal to repent from serious sins and the anger at "being told what to do" are the source of this anger. No, this sorrow is not contrition leading to repentance but a kind of anger expressed or manifested by the gnashing of teeth.

The Outer Darkness

Since heaven is lightsome and Jesus is the light of the world, here then is an image of exclusion from the presence of God. Since the heart of heaven is to be with God, the heart of hell is to be apart from Him, for whom we were made. But, in a way, unrepentant sinners get what they want after death since, as Jesus says elsewhere, they prefer the darkness (see Jn 3:19). Even so, it is still tragic that they reject the very One who alone can satisfy, preferring the darkness and the trinkets of this world.

As we have already noted, some of the most severe descriptions of hell come right from the mouth of the Lord Jesus. These are not fearmongering words of some medieval cleric drumming up business. These are the words of the sovereign Lord who loves us.

Recall, too, that the terrible anger, fiery rage, and gnawing dissipation of hell is not something unknown here on earth. Sin is disfiguring, depressing, and simmering resentment and anger that often boils over in this life. The awful futility of living apart from God's plan for us and His kingdom produces sorrow and deep frustration yet remains a stubborn disposition for the unrepentant. This world inhabited by fallen humanity tempts us daily to reject important aspects of God's plan and truth. We already know in this world how awful it is to live in the presence of many who reject God's law and vision. Hateful and murderous violence, cruelty, greed in the face of poverty, drug-lords and gangs feeding addiction and spreading violence all create unlivable hellscapes in modern cities. There is sexual confusion and depravity, abortion, treachery, and broken vows that ruin the family and violate human dignity. All this and more can make life miserable, even for those not directly involved in these sinful acts. To stubbornly persist in our own sins draws us into this hellacious world of sin. But in the real hell, there is little goodness to balance the sorrow of sins, and no grace to moderate the worst effects of sin. The whole ugly world of sin we know in this life goes on steroids in the next. Furthermore, in hell, there are no angels to guide us, no saints to encourage us, no security to protect us, and almost no virtues or the virtuous to draw forth good.

An image from St. Paul of the Cross makes this point. Imprisoned for his faith, he wrote the following passage in which he presents an image of how the very denizens of hell become one another's chief source of suffering. It is the antithesis of the communion of the saints, a kind of "chaos of the condemned."

The prison here is a true image of everlasting hell: to the cruel [physical] tortures of every kind—shackles, iron chains, manacles—are added hatred, vengeance, calumnies, obscene speech, quarrels, evil acts, swearing, curses, as well as anguish and grief. . . . How am I to bear with the spectacle, as each day I see . . . their retinue blaspheming your holy name, O Lord, who are enthroned above the Cherubim and Seraphim? Behold, the pagans have trodden your cross underfoot! Where is your glory? As I see all this, I would . . . prefer to be torn limb from limb and to die as a witness to your love. (From a letter of St. Paul Le-Bao-Tinh sent to students of the seminary of Ke-Vinh in 1843 [Paris Foreign Mission Society: Paris, 1925], pp. 80–83)

Yes, there is the real suffering of hell—selfishness, greed, hate, revenge, envy, wrath, and bitterness. It is the bad fruit of every sinful tendency amplified by the lack of repentance of the fallen and by the free and unfettered manipulation of demons. The inmates run the asylum, and to the cruelest and crudest go the spoils. It is a pretty awful picture to be sure. To suffer this fate requires a simple trajectory: stubbornly reject the kingdom of God in favor of the world of sin here and now. When death comes, the choice we made to cast our lot with this fallen world governed by a fallen angel becomes permanent. And this choice brings with it all the consequences of sin, including being in the constant company of other sinners whose choice of sin and lack of repentance are also permanently sealed. It is, as the Lord describes, a very ugly cauldron.

Hence, the Lord's vivid imagery about hell is given to us in love. His warning asks us to take seriously the choice before us. Indifference to sin grows like a metastasizing cancer in us, making repentance increasingly unlikely. We ought not dismiss His imagery. Instead, we should reverently accept that hell is a place of awful misery on account of unchecked sin. Our only reasonable response is to repent and permit Him to work His grace in us. To those with ears to hear and heed this message, the Lord adds this reassurance: "No one who calls on me will I ever reject" (Jn 6:37). So, "Seek the LORD while He may be found; call on Him while He is near. Let the wicked man forsake his own way and the unrighteous man his own thoughts; let him return to the LORD, that He may have compassion, and to our God, for He will freely pardon" (Is 55:6–7).

Other Images of Hell

Having considered our Lord's descriptions of what hell is like, we might consider just a few other accounts. Two visions in our time stand out: the vision of the children of Fatima and the vision by Sister Faustina Kwalska.

Sister Lucia and Fatima

Sister Lucia, one of the three visionaries of Fatima, wrote down in her memoirs a vision of hell that was given to them by the Virgin Mary. It describes hell as a "vast sea of fire" and was a terrifying sight to behold, especially for the three children who saw it.

[Mary] opened Her hands once more, as She had done the two previous months. The rays [of light] appeared to penetrate the earth, and we saw, as it were, a vast sea of fire. Plunged in this fire, we saw the demons and the souls [of the damned].

The latter were like transparent burning embers, all blackened or burnished bronze, having human forms. They were floating about in that conflagration, now raised into the air by the flames which issued from within themselves, together with great clouds of smoke. Now they fell back on every side like sparks in huge fires, without weight or equilibrium, amid shrieks and groans of pain and despair, which horrified us and made us tremble with fright (it must have been this sight which caused me to cry out, as people say they heard me).

The demons were distinguished [from the souls of the damned] by their terrifying and repellent likeness to frightful and unknown animals, black and transparent like burning coals. That vision only lasted for a moment, thanks to our good Heavenly Mother, Who at the first apparition had promised to take us to Heaven. Without that, I think that we would have died of terror and fear. (Lúcia de Jesus, *Fátima In Lúcia's Own Words* (1995), The Ravengate Press, pp. 101, 104)

Sister Faustina Kwalska

Sister Faustina Kwalska also wrote of the vision she had. Though most often known as a missionary of the Lord's Divine Mercy, Sister Faustina's summons of everyone to call on God's mercy is premised on the great *need* for that mercy and the awful reality of refusing that mercy. In her diary, she reports a painful vision of hell:

> I, Sister Faustina Kowalska, by the order of God, have visited the Abysses of Hell so that I might tell souls about it and testify to its existence . . . the devils were full of hatred for me, but they had to obey me at the command of God. What I have written is but a pale shadow of the things I saw. But I noticed one thing: That most of the souls there are those who disbelieve that there is a hell.
>
> I was led by an angel to the Chasms of Hell. It is a place of great torture; how awesomely large and extensive it is! The kinds of tortures I saw:
>
> The First Torture that constitutes hell is the loss of God.
>
> The Second is perpetual remorse of conscience.
>
> The Third is that one's condition will never change.
>
> The Fourth is the fire that will penetrate the soul without destroying it.
>
> The Fifth Torture is continual darkness and a terrible suffocating smell, and despite the darkness, the devils and the souls of the damned see each other and all the evil, both of others and their own.
>
> The Sixth Torture is the constant company of Satan.

The Seventh Torture is horrible despair, hatred of
God, vile words, curses and blasphemies.

These are the Tortures suffered by all the damned
together, but that is not the end of the sufferings.
There are special tortures destined for particular souls.
These are the torments of the senses. Each soul under-
goes terrible and indescribable sufferings related to
the manner in which it has sinned. There are caverns
and pits of torture where one form of agony differs
from another. I would have died at the very sight of
these tortures if the omnipotence of God had not supported me. Let the sinner know that he will be tor-
tured throughout all eternity, in those senses which he
made use of to sin. I am writing this at the command
of God, so that no soul may find an excuse by saying
there is no hell, or that nobody has ever been there,
and so no one can say what it is like . . . how terri-
bly souls suffer there! Consequently, I pray even more
fervently for the conversion of sinners. I incessantly
plead God's mercy upon them. O My Jesus, I would
rather be in agony until the end of the world, amidst
the greatest sufferings, than offend you by the least sin.
(*Diary*, 741)

There is a great similarity to Jesus's own descriptions here,
but also a development of emphasis that not all the damned
suffer in the same way. Their sufferings are connected to
the chief sin or sins which each one indulged. She speaks of
*sufferings as related to the manner in which each has sinned,
certain sufferings destined for particular souls, but not for all.*

This speaks to the justice of God wherein sufferings in hell are commensurate to the unrepented crimes on earth. Jesus surely hints at this as well when he declared that Chorazin and Bethsaida would be punished more severely than Tyre and Sidon (Mt 11:22) and that the Scribes were destined for a very strict judgment (Lk 20:47).

This teaching is generally affirmed by the Church as well. The councils of Lyon II and Florence speak of different degrees of punishment among the damned (Denzinger 858, 1306).

St. Augustine also teaches, "The lot of some of the damned will be more tolerable than that of others" (*Enchir.* 111). Theologians like St. Thomas Aquinas and lay writers and poets like Dante envision the sufferings of hell as somehow connected to one's most common and unrepented sins. And not only that, but whatever good a soul in hell may have done on earth may also lessen their suffering in hell. St. Thomas writes: "It is impossible for evil to be pure and without the admixture of good. . . . [So] those who will be thrust into hell will not be free from all good . . . those who are in hell can receive the reward of their goods, in so far as their past goods avail for the mitigation of their punishment" (*Summa Theologica*, Supplement 69.7, reply ad 9).

So, St. Thomas, answering the question "Is there any good at all in hell?" says, "Yes, there is." Hell is *not* pure evil. The reason for this is that evil is the privation or absence of something good that *should* be there. If goodness were completely absent, there would be nothing to exist. Therefore, there must be some goodness in hell or there would be nothing at all. In hell can be found the goodness of existence, intelligence in the fallen souls along with the effects of any good deeds they did while on earth that may serve to mitigate their suffering and remain part of their personality.

Note that Thomas also answers that not all the souls in hell suffer exactly alike and that the nature of suffering in hell is commensurate with the unrepented sin(s) that caused exclusion from heaven.

Dante Alighieri

Dante Alighieri (1265–1321) offers a similar but more detailed picture by presenting hell in nine different levels, with different sufferings assigned to different patterns of unrepented sin. The "Inferno" (hell) is part of his trilogy, *The Divine Comedy*. He greatly influenced the medieval imagination regarding the afterlife through this important book-length poem. It was written as a warning to the wicked to return to the path of righteousness. It follows Dante's journey through hell, purgatory, and heaven. The structure of the three realms of the afterlife follows a common pattern of nine stages plus an additional, and paramount, tenth. There are nine circles of hell, with Lucifer's dwelling place at the bottom level. There are also nine rings of purgatory, with the Garden of Eden at its peak. And there are nine celestial bodies of heaven, followed by the empyrean where God dwells.

In terms of his treatment of hell, Dante ranks the levels based on the nature of the sins and the sufferings encountered at each level. There is a kind of "poetic justice" assigned to the fallen souls that comports with their preferred sins on earth. For example, those who sinned primarily by indulging in lust and did not repent of it are in the second circle of hell. They are buffeted by the heavy winds of a violent storm without rest. This symbolizes the power of lust to blow needlessly and aimlessly and how they were carried away by their passions. The fourth circle of hell houses greedy, avaricious, or miserly hoarders and spendthrifts and those who squandered or wasted the gifts given to them by God. He sees them as literally weighed down with things, heavy weights that they roll at each other. (There is a full description of all nine circles in appendix 1.)

Dante creatively builds on the justice-based theology of St. Thomas and others wherein the souls of the damned are not all punished alike or with equal severity. Some sins are more serious than others and deserve greater punishments. As the two examples above show, there is also a kind of fittingness to the punishment. In effect, unrepentant sinners get what they want in abundance. The greedy are literally weighed down with abundance and burdened by it. The lustful have all the passion they could want, but like a driving wind, it torments them.

Another interesting feature of Dante's hell is the relative seriousness he assigns to sins. The top circles are widest and get progressively smaller (like a funnel) as they go downward. Thus, the less serious sins are more common, while the most serious are less numerous since the circles get smaller. Here is a brief description of the circles:

- **Circle 1: The unbaptized**. This kind of limbo—not really hell at all—is where God sends the unbaptized dead. While not meriting hell, they are not worthy of heaven. Instead, they live in a state of natural happiness.

- **Circle 2: The lustful.** Our Lady told the children of Fatima that the most common single reason people go to hell is unrepented sins of lust.[1] Note that Dante lists sins of lust as the least serious of sins meriting hell, but as the largest circle of hell due to its numerous denizens.

- **Circle 3: The gluttonous.** Hoarders of food, drunkards, revelers and all others who indulge to excess in the pleasures of the body.

- **Circle 4: The greedy.** The avaricious and miserly, along with hoarders and spendthrifts.

- **Circle 5: The wrathful.** The violently hateful who harbor resentment, seething indignation, and unforgiveness.

- **Circle 6: The heretics.** Those who distort God's truth and mislead others.

- **Circle 7: Violators of human life, God, and nature.** Murderers, warmongers, plunderers, tyrants, self-murderers, blasphemers, and sodomites.

- **Circle 8: The fraudulent.** Panderers and seducers, flatterers, simoniacs, sorcerers, corrupt politicians, hypocrites, thieves, counsellors of fraud, sowers of discord, schismatics, seditionists, homewreckers, falsifiers, imposters, counterfeiters, and perjurers.

---

[1] Joseph Pronechen, "On July 13, 1917, Our Lady of Fatima Showed a Vision of Hell and Taught Us How to Avoid It," *National Catholic Register*, July 13, 2017, https://www.ncregister.com/blog/on-july-13 -1917-our-lady-of-fatima-showed-a-vision-of-hell-and-taught-us-how -to-avoid-it.

- **Circle 9: The treacherous.** Betrayers of family and community ties, betrayers of guests and officials, oath breakers.
- **Center of Hell.** Here, the devil dwells, condemned for committing the ultimate sin: personal treachery against God. He is a giant, terrifying beast trapped waist-deep in the ice, fixed and suffering. He has three faces.

Dante's account of hell and his degrees of sinfulness surprise some. However, while his categorization of sins is not Church doctrine, he does largely follow the traditions of antiquity, which assign great weight to treachery and fraud since they so heavily distort human relations by undermining trust. Wrathful violence and the violation of nature, God, and others is surely also very serious. Unrepented sins of the flesh, such as lust and gluttony, while the least serious, can and do land many in hell.

Note that the experience of hell is not monolithic. God, who is just, does not indiscriminately cast those who reject His kingdom into a lake of fire. An unrepentant adulterer might not experience the same suffering in kind or degree as would a genocidal, atheistic head of state responsible for the death of millions. Both have rejected key values of the kingdom: one rejected chastity, the other rejected the worship due to God and the sacredness of human life. The magnitude of those sins is very different and so, likely, would be the consequences. While all the denizens of hell experience a kind of punishment akin to their preferred sins, by justice, it is a reasonable conclusion that the manner of their suffering varies according to the seriousness of their sins and is also likely affected by the good things they may have done, despite their ultimate rejection of God's mercy. Scripture teaches that God judges us according to our deeds (see Rom 2:6). Their good deeds may ameliorate their sufferings. Hell is not in any way pleasant, but it is not equally bad for all. Thus, God's justice, which is good, reaches even hell.

Some Thoughts from Saint Thomas Aquinas
Does God Love the Souls in Hell?

Yes. How could they continue to exist if He did not love them, sustain them, and continue to provide for them? God loves because He *is* love. Although *we* may fail to be able to experience or accept His love, God loves every being He has made, human or angelic. The souls in hell may have refused to empty their arms to receive His embrace, but God has not withdrawn His love for them. He permits those who have rejected Him to live apart from Him. God honors their freedom to say no, even respecting it when it becomes permanent, as it has for fallen angels and the souls in hell.

Do the Souls in Hell Hate God?

St. Thomas says, "No, not directly." He teaches,

> The appetite is moved by good or evil apprehended. Now God is apprehended in two ways, namely in Himself, as by the blessed, who see Him in His essence; and in His effects, as by us and by the damned. Since, then, He is goodness by His essence, He cannot in

Himself be displeasing to any will; wherefore whoever sees Him in His essence cannot hate Him.

On the other hand, some of His effects are displeasing to the will in so far as they are opposed to anyone: and accordingly, a person may hate God not in Himself, but by reason of His effects. Therefore, the damned, perceiving God in His punishment, which is the effect of His justice, hate Him, even as they hate the punishment inflicted on them (*Summa Theologica*, Supplement, q. 98, art. 5).

Do the Souls in Hell Wish They Were Dead or Desire No Longer to Exist?

Here, too, St. Thomas answers, "No." It is impossible to detest what is fundamentally good, and "to exist" is fundamentally good. Those who say that they "wish they were dead" do not really wish nonexistence upon themselves. Rather, they wish an end to their suffering. So, it is with the souls in hell, even as for some of us on earth. St. Thomas teaches,

> Not "to be" may be considered in two ways. First, in itself, and thus it can nowise be desirable, since it has no aspect of good, but is pure privation of good. Secondly, it may be considered as a relief from a painful life or from some unhappiness: and thus "not to be" takes on the aspect of good, since "to lack an evil is a kind of good" as the Philosopher says (Ethic. v, 1). In this way it is better for the damned not to be than to be unhappy. Hence it is said (Matthew 26:24): "It were better for him, if that man had not been born," and

(Jeremiah 20:14): "Cursed be the day wherein I was born," where a gloss of Jerome observes: "It is better not to be than to be evilly." In this sense the damned can prefer "not to be" according to their deliberate reason (*Summa Theologica*, Supplement, q. 98, art. 3).

And a Final Insight from Archbishop Fulton Sheen

And finally, we might ponder the essential suffering at the root of hell, a suffering common to every level of hell. Most will believe it is separation from God, for whom we were all made and apart from whom we cannot rest or find peace. This truth, however, is not immediately obvious to those who have rejected God. For them, one way to explain this mystery is to say that being in hell is like missing the one thing necessary. For instance, it is like owning a mansion without a key or keeping a fortune in a bank account without the PIN. It would be better not to have riches that are out of reach. Along these lines, Archbishop Sheen told the following parable about hell:

> There is not a golfer in America who has not heard the story, which is theologically sound, about the golfer who went to Hell and asked to play golf. The Devil showed him a 36-hole course with a beautiful clubhouse, long fairways, perfectly placed hazards, rolling hills, and velvety greens. Next, the Devil gave him a set of clubs so well balanced that the golfer felt he had been swinging them all his life. Out to the first tee they

stepped, ready for a game. The golfer said, "What a course! Give me the ball." The Devil answered: "Sorry, we have no golf balls in Hell. That's the hell of it!" (*Three to Get Married*, Kindle Edition, Loc. 851–57)

A Subtle but Piercing Description of Hell

Perhaps hell has its "goods," but there is no way to enjoy them! Many are surprised to think that there could be anything "good" in hell at all. But, as noted, evil is the privation of good; if demons, the damned, and hell itself had *nothing* good, they would not exist at all! There is no such thing as pure evil, for it would be pure nothing. So, perhaps there are good things in hell, but the key to enjoying them is missing!

God, of course, is the key to unlocking every other good. Having rejected the vision of God for their life, the damned lack the "one thing necessary" to unlock every other blessing. The frustration of this is but a more intense version of what many now experience as they try to satisfy their infinite longings in a finite world. It doesn't work. We have a God-size hole in our heart, and only God can fill it. Until we learn this lesson and set our sights on Him, we will be frustrated and unfulfilled. If we refuse to admit our need for Him before we die, we will lack forever the one blessing necessary to unlock every other blessing. Saint Augustine well described this truth in his *Confessions*. There is the memorable line: "You have made us for Yourself, and our hearts are restless until they rest in You" (*Confessions*, Book 1:1.1).

Only grace and mercy can rescue us from Satan's seductive lies. Run to Jesus, repenting of your sins. Ask for the grace to recognize the awful reality of hell, with all its sledge-hammer force and its somber subtleties. Ask for the grace to see through the lies to the lasting truth of the glory of heaven. And above all, do not dismiss the warning of Jesus that many are on the wide road to damnation, while few are on the narrow road to salvation. The Lord loves us and wants to save us, but He needs our "yes." Say "yes" to Him every day! An old gospel song says:

> Yes, Lord, yes, Lord,
> From the bottom of my heart
> To the depths of my soul.
> Yes, Lord, completely yes.
> My soul says yes.[2]

---

[2] *Completely Yes* by Sandra Crouch.

Chapter 8

Why the Doctrine of Hell Matters

If You Don't Know the Bad News, the Good News Is No News

As with any doctrine, the teaching on hell intersects with other teachings by either supporting them or being supported by them. Let's consider what the largely empty hell of universalism does to other teachings of the Church and Scriptures.

Soteriology Is Undermined

The doctrine of hell is not an esoteric and merely academic matter. It goes to the very heart of God's plan for our salvation. The Church refers to the theology of salvation as "soteriology." This is rooted in a Greek word, "soter," which means "savior." But the practical denial of hell, by relegating it to anything but a very remote possibility, has the effect of removing the need for a savior. At best, Jesus becomes an ethical teacher or wise counsellor. At worst, He becomes wholly irrelevant. But the fundamental and saving call of the Lord, "Repent and believe the Gospel!" (Mk 1:15) moves from being a clarion call of plenary authority and decisive importance to "something nice to consider if you can find time to get around to it." Jesus has come to save us, but we must first admit we need saving, and this work can only be accomplished by Him. Either we believe in Him and are saved or we reject His teachings and are lost (cf. Mk 16:16; Jn 3:18; 8:24; 14:6; Mt 21:32ff; Jn 10:26; 5:38; inter al).

Vast Amounts of Scripture Are Ignored

The doctrine of hell, based on the repeated biblical assertions of Jesus that many are heading there and fewer find heaven, must be accepted at face value. When Jesus says few are on the narrow road to heaven, "few" does not mean many or most; it means *few*. Hell is not a remote possibility based on the frequent warnings of Jesus and the many admonitions of the apostles who speak for Him. Furthermore, the modern tendency to dismiss the evidence is unfaithful to Scripture and dismissive of the most central concern of Jesus.

The Plan and Medicines of Salvation Are Trivialized

The denial or diminishment of hell makes God and His teaching superfluous. Everything of God—His law, knowledge of Scripture, sacred liturgy, sacraments, prayer, catechesis, evangelization, missionaries, or even Church membership— no longer matters. If heaven is in the bag for the vast majority of humanity, the work of the Church becomes merely a sociological structure for people to socialize in community; she is no longer necessary for salvation, and her sacraments become mere ceremonies that set the stage for a nice party in the afterlife.

It is no surprise that Mass attendance has declined at the same time the doctrine of hell is widely dismissed, even by Church leaders. There is no urgency to repent since the salvation of souls has become an afterthought. People who think they are well don't go to the doctor. Even more, who would go to a doctor whose diagnosis of every perceived ailment is always rosy and who says every time, "Nothing to see here . . . Nothing to fear"? And yet, that is precisely what most Catholics, including our leaders, have done. By denying the consequences of sin and the need for repentance, we have consigned ourselves to irrelevancy. The Church has become, in many places, little more than a social club where all are welcome.

The Missionary Zeal of the Church Is Lessened

Missionaries once made great sacrifices when they traveled to far-flung regions to preach the Gospel because they thought that, without the Lord, people in those regions might reasonably be lost and that they, like anyone else, needed the truth of the Gospel and grace to make it through this dark world to the kingdom of light and life. Were they wrong? Of course not. But with our strange and unbiblical stance on hell, we more than imply they were wrong, or at least exaggerated the urgency of the endeavor.

The Virtue of Hope Is Undermined

Hope is confident expectation of God's help in attaining eternal life. But, as St. Paul says, "Who hopes for what he already has?" (Rom 8:24). If you have already won a race,

why hope to win what you already have? And St. Thomas
Aquinas says that hope spurs us to seek a good that is difficult but possible.[3] But if heaven is easy to attain and most
do, who really needs the virtue of hope? And yet, hope is so
important that God offers it as a supernatural and theological virtue. And why did St. Paul say, "But I discipline my
body and keep it under control, lest after preaching to others
I myself should be disqualified" (1 Cor 9:27)? If heaven is the
destination of most people, while hell is sparsely populated
if occupied at all, why do this? So, hope is rendered largely
meaningless and unnecessary by the universalist notions that
all are saved. Hans Urs von Balthasar's question (and book)
Dare We Hope That All Men Be Saved? has the strange effect
of cancelling hope in the very act of hoping. It is a strange
utterance. Hope as a virtue stands between despair (a defect
of hope) and presumption (an excess of hope). Like all virtues, hope provides the balance that orthodoxy requires
wherein we accept the Lord's teaching that salvation is a hard
and narrow road that relatively few find, and the other truth
that God wants to save us, and we need not fear but confidently turn to Him for grace and mercy. Hope understands
the grim condition of the human heart and our tendency to
prefer the darkness of sin but moves forward with the confident expectation of God's help to see our hearts changed and
our desires converted. And since hope contains the premise
that the task is difficult though possible, we remain reverent
and humble before God, knowing that the remedies required
by God are urgently needed and necessary.

---

[3]   *Summa Theologicae* II-II, q. 17, a. 1.

The Error of Universalism Undermines Joy

As has been noted above, "If you don't know the bad news, the good news is no news." Given all the bad news noted above about concupiscence, sloth, disordered passions, lukewarmness, and the tendency to prefer the darkness to the light, it is awesomely good news that God can still break through all these vices to save us! The Lord said to St. Faustina, "Do not be frightened at this [but] If I were to reveal to you the whole misery that you are, you would die of terror. . . . But because you are such great misery I have revealed to you the whole ocean of my mercy" (*Diary*, II. 718).

Wow. Thank God for mercy and run to Him with joy, realizing how much you need it and won't make it without Him. But as the parable of the man who owed a huge debt teaches (Mt 18:21–35), there is a strange lack of awareness of what God has done for us and how awful we are apart from Him. The man in the parable had an immense debt (20,000 talents!) that he could never hope to repay. His fate was sealed. When the king forgives his whole debt, one would expect that he would dance for joy, issuing forth in gratitude, generosity, kindness, and forgiveness. Yet strangely, he walks blithely away and seems unmoved. When a small debtor cannot pay him, he imposes severe penalties on the poor man. What happened to him was what didn't happen to him. It didn't seem to occur to him just how awful his condition was and that his only real destination was going to be prison or slavery. He seemed anesthetized from reality and so, when salvation was offered, his joy was lacking. He didn't know the bad news, so the good news was no news.

And what of us in this age of Universalism? Is joy evident on Christian faces? Are we profoundly grateful for what the Lord has done for us? We were dead in our sins, destined for hell with no hope. St. Paul says,

> And you he made alive, when you were dead through the trespasses and sins in which you once walked, following the course of this world, following the prince of the power of the air, the spirit that is now at work in the sons of disobedience. Among these we all once lived in the passions of our flesh, following the desires of body and mind, and so we were by nature children of wrath, like the rest of mankind. But God, who is rich in mercy, out of the great love with which he loved us, even when we were dead through our trespasses, made us alive together with Christ (by grace you have been saved), and raised us up with him, and made us sit with him in the heavenly places in Christ Jesus, that in the coming ages he might show the immeasurable riches of his grace in kindness toward us in Christ Jesus. For by grace you have been saved through faith; and this is not your own doing, it is the gift of God—not because of works, lest any man should boast. For we are his workmanship, created in Christ Jesus for good works, which God prepared beforehand, that we should walk in them. (Eph 2:1–10)

Wow! Without God, we were lost, and without accepting His grace now, we are without hope. Fortunately, He can save us from the mess we are and the mess we have made! But what if none of this is true? What if it didn't matter what spiritual condition you were in, and those who lived in sin were never really in danger of total loss at all? What happens to the joy of salvation? It is never set loose because there isn't any real threat after all. The vast majority are and always have been on the road to heaven. No need, therefore, to strike up a *Te Deum* or sing long alleluias. No bad news means no good news either, just a big ho hum.

Does universalism also help explain our often-joyless times and the boredom that afflicts us, even in our worship? Perhaps so. Those who know joy best have been to the precipice of danger and also know the depths of sin and sorrow. For them, the rescue is real and the urgency to stay close to God and save others is clearer. Universalism is bland, but orthodoxy highlights the drama before us: blessing or curse, life or death (cf. Dt 30:19) and conveys the joy that God has given us a hope and opened a way to the Father and to heaven by the opening in the veil of Christ's flesh (Heb 10).

So, while the teaching that many are on the road to destruction may cause fear, it can also cause a joyful resolve to stay close to the Lord who alone can save us from the greatest enemy of all, our very selves!

Universalism Diminishes the Freedom at the Heart of Human Dignity

At the heart of human dignity is our freedom—that is, the use of our intellect and will as moral agents. We are differentiated from the animals, many of whom possess mammalian physicality but lack a spiritual soul capable of thought and free decisions. The animals and all creatures of

God's kingdom interact with the physical world and follow instincts. But the human person can perceive and interact with the metaphysical world (from the Greek *meta*, meaning "beyond," and *phusis*, meaning "physical"). We perceive not only physical realities, such as trees, birds, etc., but also metaphysical realities, such as justice, honor, meaning, purpose, and so forth. We can grasp not only concepts such as efficient and material causality but also formal and final causality (concepts related to the purpose and end of things). This demonstrates the distinctiveness and glory of humanity.

But many modern notions erode this dignity and enslave us to our passions. We become, in our habitual and irrational lack of control, too weak and too stupid to ever merit hell or most of the consequences of our sins.

Mere decades ago, youth of eighteen to twenty-five years stormed the beaches of Normandy to deliver a decisive blow to Nazi Germany. Today, the same age group is considered, practically speaking, incapable of entering the life-long vow of marriage. What changed: human nature or our understanding of it? Surely the latter. We live in a kind of "therapeutic" culture wherein many, if not most, people are said to have PTSD, ADHD, alcoholism, sexual addiction, autism, and a host of many other "spectrums." It is said that these things render us incapable of making the free decisions for which we are responsible. As such, hell is not a possible destination for a generation incapable of free, intelligent, and mature decisions. It is a sad reduction of the human person to the status of a high school sophomore.

Yet, even in our time, people who suffer from addiction and other disabilities have demonstrated an ability to defeat their demons. Alcoholics Anonymous, for example, still presumes that human beings can decide to change. Though difficult and confounded with what they often call "stinkin' thinkin,'" alcoholics are summoned to freedom and a decisive break with the lie that they cannot stop drinking: "We admitted we were powerless over alcohol and that our lives had become unmanageable and came to believe that a Power greater than ourselves could restore us to sanity."[4] Is it possible that there is more faith in the church basement at an AA meeting than in the marriage tribunals of the Catholic Church? You decide. But sadly, this vigorous notion is lacking today among many Catholic theologians and clergy who too easily conclude that human beings are not able to reason morally and/or are too weak to overcome their passions.

Catholic moral theology does teach that ignorance or the passions can lessen the guilt or blameworthiness of sins. Yes, the Lord does account for ignorance, but it is not a *carte blanche* for all the poorly catechized. But too often this has become the baseline or presumed norm rather than a factor that is more the exception than the rule. We have also identified many reasons in chapter 4 why the road to hell is a common path and that most people are not "too stupid to go to hell." Most know quite well what they are doing and when it is right or wrong, and if they prefer light or darkness.

The fashionable notion that hell is a remote possibility or even empty undermines human dignity by presupposing that human ignorance and enslavement to passion makes meaningful or lasting decisions impossible. A further implication

---

[4]   AA Steps 1 and 2.

is that grace cannot adequately aid suffering humanity. This thinking also undermines the utility of moral exhortation, rendering the moral life a kind of unrealistic aspiration, or one to which we are not ultimately accountable. None of this is acceptable, of course, and universalism both flows from this mentality and further fuels it.

Universalism Removes a Crucial Remedy for Sin and Vengeance

Remembering that we will one day have to render an account to God for what we have done is an important curb on human sinfulness. In a culture of increasing unbelief and practical atheism like ours, so few people realize that one day they will have to answer to God for what they have done. This spiritual neglect cannot be helpful to human conduct or good order. Universalism feeds this attitude, even among believers, that we must one answer to God and that our unrepented sins can have eternal consequences. If hell is a remote possibility, an important motivation to repent and choose well is lost. This point is particularly relevant to the problem of vengeance. St. Paul rightly cautioned the faithful against vengeance, writing, "Do not avenge yourselves, beloved, but leave room for God's wrath. For it is written: 'Vengeance is Mine; I will repay, says the Lord'" (Rom 12:19). So, all of us will answer to God for what we have done. And those who have harmed us, often in terrible ways and without repentance, will answer to God for what they have done. But without this assurance of final justice, many today might be tempted to avenge themselves, often employing violence that overflows and intensifies. Let's be honest. Few of us are motivated to behave well without the firm possibility of lasting punishments. And many of us grow bitter and cynical when serious crimes and criminals go unpunished. We see this in our culture now, and Universalism can seem to remove a final appeal to perfect justice. There is the paradoxical result that a lack of final and perfect justice also harms God's mercy. For many could rightfully ask what kind of mercy is there when unrepentant evildoers are waved into heaven along with their victims. True mercy requires justice; removing justice harms mercy.

Summary

To deny the scriptural teaching of the Lord on hell as a real possibility for many undermines just about everything else we teach, say, or do. This includes our most central and miraculous teaching that the Lord has saved us by His perfect sacrifice and offers that salvation to everyone. Saved us? Saved us from what? Something that was already in the bag for most of us? Who will weep for joy over something that they never knew was lost or could be easily lost? If we are no longer saved from the consequences of sin, the gospel message of salvation becomes irrelevant and incoherent. And this is no mere speculation. Empty churches signal that we failed to communicate any pressing need for the Gospel, for grace, for sacraments, Scripture, or prayer. While numbers should not be an obsession for us, they illustrate our failure to reach the vast majority of souls in the West. In the COVID shutdowns, government officials said churches were less essential than liquor stores and casinos, which stayed open, while houses of worship were ordered closed. And, frankly, our Church leaders were more than willing to comply. Having removed any major catastrophe such as hell from preaching at Mass, we are left confused about the purpose of the Church. And the faithful have heard the message. For most Catholics, it matters little whether they go to Mass or not, receive sacraments or not, pray and study Scripture or not. If members of the household lack any zeal or urgency, how will the world respond? If the trumpet sounds an uncertain call, who will prepare for battle? (see 1 Cor 14:8). Salvation is meaningless if there is nothing to be saved from, and the good news of the gospel about the most pivotal event of all human history, the passion, death, and resurrection of Christ, falls on deaf ears.

Some may say our current state is largely one of invincible ignorance and that this is the reason we can now conclude hell is empty or a remote possibility. But that is not realistic. Any honest look at the injustice, greed, lust, cruelty, and generally debased condition of this world leads to the conclusion that too many choose darkness over light. The only proper and urgent response is strong moral exhortation and preaching rooted in the word of God, regular reception of the Sacraments, and attendance at the holy liturgy. We must recover the full doctrine of hell, not as a pretext to keep people fearful but to remain faithful to what the Lord actually teaches. And He teaches this because it is true, and He loves us enough to warn us that a very real danger is ever-present and requires our constant "yes" to the work He must accomplish to save us. In the next chapter, we will ponder some elements of this lost doctrine that must be recovered. But for now, consider two texts that warn us against feigning ignorance:

> For if the message declared by angels was valid and every transgression or disobedience received a just retribution, how shall we escape if we neglect such a great salvation? It was declared at first by the Lord, and it was attested to us by those who heard him, while God also bore witness by signs and wonders and various miracles and by gifts of the Holy Spirit distributed according to his own will. (Heb 2:2–4)

> See that you do not refuse him who is speaking. For if they did not escape when they refused him who warned them on earth, much less shall we escape if we reject him who warns from heaven. (Heb 12:25)

Chapter 9

Recovering the Doctrine of Hell

How to Speak of Hell in a Clear and Pastoral Way

This brief reflection has shown that the doctrine of hell is not some dark medieval teaching rooted in fear. Rather, it is a central aspect of Jesus's own teaching and preaching. He mentions it over and over. Most of the parables are devoted to our coming judgment and the strong risk that many do not make it into heaven. Most of the teaching on hell, even the most fearsome and shocking descriptions, come right from the mouth of Jesus, the one who loves us. We cannot remain faithful to His words if we minimize and downplay them by hoping they were spoken insincerely or mean something else because we want to believe that hell is empty. Such thoughts, while understandable, have caused great harm in the Body of Christ, as we pondered in the last chapter, by deflating evangelization and rendering nearly the whole mission and message of the Church incoherent and thus irrelevant.

All this said, it remains a challenge for us today to reclaim the proper doctrine of hell in a way that avoids caricatures and responds effectively to the objections of doubters. The possibility of a hell that is fiery and eternal, dark, and filled with suffering does seem to many at odds with a loving and merciful God. Further, do many realize what they are doing? Does not ignorance play a role in lessening numbers? And are we really free enough to be held accountable for our many bad choices?

Some answers have already been proposed in the pages of this book. But let's consider some basic points which summarize these answers by way of review and conclusion.

Hell Exists Because God Respects Human Freedom

As developed in chapter 2, hell does not exist because God is angry and vengeful. Hell exists because God has deep respect for the freedom of every human person. Beginning with the Garden of Eden, God offered man a choice to love Him or not. The freedom to answer this call is our dignity and a necessary aspect of our vocation to love. There cannot be love if the decision to love is forced or has no real alternative. Jesus describes Himself as standing at the door of our heart and knocking (see Rv 3:20). He does not barge in and force Himself or His kingdom upon us. Our freedom to answer is very real and bestows on us dignity *and* responsibility. Simply put, do we want the Lord and His kingdom of light, or do we prefer the darkness? Sadly, as Jesus teaches, many prefer the darkness. Hell exists, first and foremost, because we are free, and many freely choose the darkness (see Jn 3:19*ff*).

Not All Want What God Offers

Some believe almost everyone wants what God offers since everyone wants to go to heaven. But, as already noted in chapter 2, this is not really true. Rather, many want a kind of designer paradise, a heaven on their own terms. But the real heaven is on God's terms and includes what God loves and who God loves. Many do not like key elements of God's kingdom, such as forgiveness, chastity, love of one's enemy, and worship. God will not force us to love what or who He loves. This is obvious today since many of God's teachings and values are scorned by doubters as intolerant, unreasonable, outdated, and even hateful. Many indeed hate the truth and thus see the truth as hateful. God sends graces and messengers of His truth, but He does not force compliance. For those who die unrepentant, God grants them a place apart where the darkness they prefer and the sins they cling to are present in abundance. It is not a pleasant place, but it is what they want in the place of the real heaven. In the end, you get what you want, and it is a sad reality that many (not few) do not want what God is offering. To some extent, heaven is an acquired taste. To desire what He offers, God must heal our worldly wounded hearts. Sadly, only a few are willing to let Him perform heart surgery. Be among that few!

God Is Not Angry

Chapter 5 was devoted to the wrath of God. Recall that wrath does not refer to God's anger. Rather, wrath is our human experience of the total incompatibility of our sinful state in the presence of God's profound holiness. We simply cannot endure His presence if we are steeped in sin. It is like fire and water; they do not mix, and there will be conflict if they come together. One can hear the wrathful conflict if water is dropped on a hot stove. Hence, prior to our judgment, it is necessary for God to change us since God cannot change. We must permit Him to prepare us for heaven. He accomplishes this in many ways through His grace, the sacraments, the holy liturgy, prayer, Scripture, and through our sufferings and other purifications. So the Lord does not want us to experience this "wrath," but He must engage in a work to help us avoid this fate. Scripture says, "For God has not appointed us to suffer wrath, but to obtain salvation through our Lord Jesus Christ" (1 Thes 5:9). "Indeed, Jesus is our deliverer from the coming wrath" (1 Thes 1:10). So, once again, the problem is not God; it is us. We need to choose the Lord and let Him do his saving work. But the choice is ours. Choose Jesus and heaven!

Are We Free and Knowledgeable Enough to Choose Hell?

The answer to this question must ultimately be yes. If not, the entire moral exhortation of the Scriptures would be pointless and its warnings against sin would be downright cruel. The stance of God and His Church is to engage the human person as a moral agent who is free to make responsible decisions.

And as to having sufficient knowledge to make individual and existential choices, we know what we are doing in most cases. We have a conscience and a grasp of basic moral principles. Since God is just, He will account for invincible ignorance, but as noted, this is not a blank check. And, as the Second Vatican Council notes,

Nor does Divine Providence deny the helps necessary for salvation to those who, without blame on their part, have not yet arrived at an explicit knowledge of God and with His grace strive to live a good life. Whatever good or truth is found amongst them is looked upon by the Church as a preparation for the Gospel. . . . But often men, deceived by the Evil One, have become vain in their reasonings and have exchanged the truth of God for a lie, serving the creature rather than the Creator. Or some there are who, living and dying in this world without God, are exposed to final despair. Wherefore to promote the glory of God and procure the salvation of all of these, and mindful of the command of the Lord, "Preach the Gospel to every creature," the Church fosters the missions with care and attention. (*Lumen Gentium*, 16)

To quickly presume ignorance upon the vast majority of humanity is to diminish human dignity. While we leave the question of invincible ignorance to God, we ought to recall that Jesus, who will judge us, said that few were on the road to salvation and did not add, "except for the vast majority of humanity who never heard enough to make a real decision one way or the other." How God handles this is up to Him. We ought not, then, make that decision ourselves and become too presumptive. God does not express grave doubts about our freedom or knowledge. Rather, He treats us as if we can make responsible choices. God will make just exceptions to this baseline at His discretion. It is not for us to engage in sinful presumption by issuing blank checks that God has not signed.

The faithful reply to God's teaching is a sober acceptance that there is a hell and that many (not few) prefer the darkness to the light and freely and knowingly persist in this stance. Our proper stance should be one of sober urgency, calling souls to conversion, starting with our own.

Hell Is for the Unrepentant

Jesus states clearly, "No one who calls on me will I reject" (Jn 6:37). Therefore, hell is not for repentant sinners but for those who are stubborn and refuse to repent. Sadly, today they are legion. Vast numbers of people have drifted from the faith; some have apostatized, and quite often they publicly oppose many of the teachings of the Lord and His Church. Most often, this puts them in a state of rebellion. Scripture describes many of them: "Although they know God's righteous decree that those who do such things are worthy of death, they not only continue to do these things, but also approve of those who practice them" (Rom 1:32). Yes, many today fit this description.

Hell is the probable destination for these unrepentant sinners.

A Sin Against the Holy Spirit

In effect, their sin against the Holy Spirit becomes unforgivable. St. Thomas Aquinas enumerates six species or kinds of sin against the Holy Spirit:

1. **Despair:** Complete abandonment of hope in God's help to overcome sin.

2. **Presumption:** Being overconfident of God's help and mercy without any work on our part, especially through repentance.

3. **Impugning the Known Truth:** Willfully distorting, attacking, or contradicting a teaching of God we know to be true.

4. **Envy of Another's Spiritual Good:** Seeking to destroy the good in others because we take it to lessen our standing.

5. **Obstinacy in Sin:** Stubbornly refusing God's graces to fight and overcome our sins and vices. This includes indulging in ignorance.

6. **Final Impenitence:** A persistent and explicit rejection of God's mercy by the refusal to repent or admit the need for forgiveness.

As can be seen, numbers three, five, and six are very common sins. Many do not tolerate sound doctrine but consult "teachers" who say what they want to hear. Many also stubbornly persist in sin; they refuse correction and call it hate. They refuse mercy and claim they don't need it. God is always urging every human person, baptized or not, to seek Him and repent of their transgressions. The souls in hell did not just have bad luck, perhaps lacking an eloquent and effective call to repent. They resisted the Holy Spirit and the many graces of God bestowed not only on the baptized but on every human person.

The mystery of this unrepentance is caught up in the mystery of iniquity. But, that said, it is not hard to realize that mercy cannot be imposed; it must be offered and freely accepted. Suppose someone came to you and said, "I forgive you for all the terrible things you said to me yesterday." But suppose further that you did not think you said terrible things yesterday, but things that were true and needed to be said. In this example, the offer of mercy seems odious and manipulative. Hence, mercy cannot be imposed. Repentance, the admission that one has sinned, is the key that must unlock mercy. Sadly, to the unrepentant, talk of God's mercy seems judgmental and harsh, and they reject it when they refuse to repent. They sin against the Holy Spirit, who always urges us to love God and repent of our sins. As such, they inherit hell not as the angry penalty of a wrathful God but as a respectful and loving God who honors their freedom, giving them what they want. The judgment issues forth in a ruling so sorrowfully spoken by Jesus, "And this is the verdict: The Light has come into the world, but men loved the darkness rather than the Light because their deeds were evil" (Jn 3:19).

Epilogue

"The beginning of wisdom is the Fear of the Lord."

—Proverbs 9:10

"If anyone is ashamed of Me and My words, the Son of Man will be ashamed of him when He comes in His glory and in the glory of the Father and of the holy angels."

—Luke 9:26

In times like these, when the doctrine of hell is all but excluded from the minds of most, even among many pious Catholics, what are we to do? Strongly connected to the rejection of the biblical teachings on hell is the trivializing and "taming" of God. He is, for too many, merely kind rather than immensely holy and glorious beyond telling. There is little notion that we must be utterly transformed and perfected to attain the glory that is our future and destiny if we are faithful unto the end. As noted previously, Scripture says, "It is a fearful thing to fall into the hands of the living God" (Heb 10:31). And again, it says we must "Strive for the holiness, without which no one will see the Lord" (Heb 12:14).

A proper balance must be restored to us, which trusts God's mercy but acknowledges how very much we need it; a balance which knows and experiences God's love but which also holds Him in awe and deep reverence. This virtuous balance is what Scripture calls "the fear of the Lord." The fear of the Lord holds God in awe and reverently loves Him. It dreads offending Him and anything that might separate us from Him. Ideally, it is rooted in deep gratitude and love, which fears to offend Him because of His goodness to us. In those who are less spiritually mature, it may well include the servile fear of punishment. But at its best, it manifests as an excited and joyful reverence in God's presence, amazed at His glory and humbly aware of our need for His grace and mercy.

To fear the Lord is also to accept His teaching without reserve, even if it puzzles us or causes alarm. The Lord Jesus loves us more than we can ever know and is rich in mercy, but He expects to be taken seriously. The gift of the fear of the Lord must therefore be sought by us and cherished. Without it we too easily trivialize the Lord and accept him only on our terms. It is true, Jesus is the Lover of our souls, He has born our sins, and opened to us the ocean of His mercy. But this same Jesus spoke to us very plainly of the reality of Hell. He also teaches us that we are very fickle and perverse of heart. Take Him seriously in these matters! In holy fear and deep reverence listen to what He is saying and be urgent about the salvation of souls, starting with your own. A Day of Judgement is coming for all of us, and the choice is ours: "And this is the verdict: The Light has come into the world, but men loved the darkness rather than the Light" (Jn 3:19).

Be urgent and choose wisely, fellow sinner. Listen to Jesus and come to the light. Respectful of our freedom, He knocks at our door and waits joyfully and expectantly for us to open. You are free to choose, but you are *not* free not to choose.

Dante's Inferno: A Summary of the Circles

Dante envisioned nine concentric circles of hell. The nine circles are really levels moving toward the center of the Earth, representing increasing degrees of wickedness. At the lowest or innermost circle is the center of the Earth, where Satan is imprisoned in a paradoxical sea of ice, frozen up to his waist and strangely bored. Most notably, the sinners in each circle are experiencing punishments befitting their crimes. As noted, this exemplifies God's justice. Not all those in hell are punished in the same way or with equal intensity. Each receives a kind of "just desserts" or "poetic justice" in which the sins they preferred to heaven become theirs in abundance in hell.

Dante's vision of hell was not entirely original. He based his ideas on ancient sources such as Aristotle and Cicero. Virgil, who leads Dante on this tour of hell, reminds the Italian poet of Aristotle's *Ethics*, wherein hell was divided into three major categories: incontinence, vice, and brute bestiality. Dante adapts these to incontinence, violence (bestiality), and fraud. From here, we see the following structure of hell:

First Circle (Limbo)

This is not hell *per se*, and thus the first circle is not enumerated among the nine circles of hell. In this limbo are the unbaptized and virtuous pagans who, although not sinful enough to warrant damnation, did not accept Christ. It is a kind of lesser form of heaven.

Second Circle (Lust)

It is described as "a part where nothing gleams." In the second circle of hell are those who primarily indulged in lust and refused to repent. They face the terrible winds of a violent storm without rest. This symbolizes the power of lust to blow needlessly and aimlessly, so that they are carried away by their passions. Since lust is not wholly self-centered and involves mutual indulgence, Dante believes it is less serious than other sins, and its punishment is the "lightest" within hell's circles.

Third Circle (Gluttony)

The gluttonous allowed their passion for food, drink, and other bodily pleasures and appetites to go uncontrolled. Now they are stuck in a slush of putrefaction. Dante sees them as groveling in this mire by themselves, sightless and heedless of their neighbors. Gluttony includes not only overindulgence in food and drink but also other kinds of excess.

Fourth Circle (Greed)

In this circle are those whose greed became a dominant part of their lives. They insisted on material excess since they were never satisfied, and we can assume they were insensitive to the needy and poor. Dante lists a variety of occupants: the avaricious and the miserly, hoarders and spendthrifts, and those who squander or waste things. He describes their punishment as being literally weighed down with things. And they taunt each other: "Why do you hoard?" "Why do you waste?" The self-centered become hyper-aware that others might have more or be wasting what could be theirs.

Fifth Circle (Wrath)

Here are the violently angry and hateful, joined by those whose anger took a more passive-aggressive form. The violently wrathful fight each other viciously on the surface of slime, while the sullen and passively wrathful lie beneath the water, withdrawn, in a black depression without joy or humor. In life, they likely indulged their anger and sullen resentment because it made them feel righteous and superior to those they thought had harmed them. Refusing God's gift of forgiveness, they now have all the anger they could ever want.

Sixth Circle (Heresy)

In the sixth circle, heretics, such as Epicurus and his followers (who say "the soul dies with the body"), are trapped in flaming tombs. The heretics are in hell for warping and misrepresenting the faith and misleading others.

Seventh Circle (Violence)

This circle is divided into three rings:

Ring 1

Violence against neighbors: the murderers, warmongers, plunderers, and tyrants. They now drown in boiling blood forever, each according to the degree of his guilt.

Ring 2

Violence against self: suicides, those who rejected suffering and could not trust God to see them through.

Ring 3

Violence against God, art, and nature: ere are blasphemers (who sin against God), the sodomites (who sin against nature), and the usurers (who sin against the arts and industries of men by inflating prices). They all suffer in the hot desert they helped to create literally and figuratively on earth (see Gn 19:24).

Eighth Circle (Fraud)

The eighth circle is an image of a corrupt city. Here are those who corrupted every relationship, personal and public. There are:

- Panderers and seducers: who deliberately exploited others for their own profit. They are whipped by horned demons for eternity.

- Flatterers: who exploited and played upon the weaknesses and fears of others regarding status. They are standing in excrement and fight among themselves.
- Simoniacs: who sold Church favors and offices, making money for themselves from what belongs to God. They are placed, head down, in ugly replicas of baptismal fonts.
- Sorcerers: those who were fortune tellers, diviners, astrologers, and other false prophets; those who sought to look into the future which is for God to know. Their heads are backwards on their bodies. Since they tried to see into the future, now they cannot even see in front of themselves and walk backwards.
- Corrupt politicians: who made money by corruption of public offices. They are immersed in a lake of boiling pitch symbolizing their sticky fingers and dark deals.
- Hypocrites: who hid their true selves from others and pretended to be what they were not. Now they are weighed down by lead robes showing the weight of his deception.
- Thieves: who stole other people's substance in life. Now their very self becomes subject to theft as monstrous reptiles bite at their flesh and curl themselves about these thieves.
- Evil and false counsellors: who promote conflict and thereby tore apart what God intended to unite. They are Church schismatics, those who caused civil conflicts and political divisions, and those who divided

families and tribes. Now they move about hidden from view, with no influence, inside a wall of flames.

- Falsifiers: the imposters, counterfeiters, and perjurers. They run about as if they were fleeing from their lies.

Ninth Circle (Treachery)

Here, trapped in a large frozen lake, are sinners punished for treachery against those with whom they had special relationships. Here are those who sinned against family ties, community ties, unsuspecting guests, and against God and country. Dante assigns to treachery the deepest pit of hell. Consider well that to turn on those we should love the most is very serious. Loyalty and perseverance are essential to the human community. Treachery stabs at the heart of the ties that should bind and endangers the pillar and fabric of faith and family.

At the very center of hell is the devil. He has three faces and, unexpectedly, is trapped in waist-deep ice. He seems bored and almost unaware of Virgil and Dante as he gnaws on Judas Iscariot.

Hence, we see from Dante a rather gruesome description of hell, arrayed according to the most common sins committed by its "citizens." As can be seen, these sins are sadly common throughout humanity and human history. Some of the many sins described here are dismissed or simply forgotten by many. Note, for example, how treachery, deemed most serious by Dante and assigned to the lowest circle of hell, is seldom mentioned. The punishments for all the unrepented sins described are allotted in different measures according to their seriousness. And this is a picture of God's justice. It is conceived by Dante and others according to reason and a kind of poetic license. These things are not detailed in Scripture, which speaks only in a general way of fiery sufferings. But such an analysis by Dante and others, such as St. Thomas Aquinas, rely on the use of reason, which applies God's justice to divine reward and punishment in the afterlife. Thus, such descriptions are not purely speculative or fanciful theology. Rather, they seek to apply known truths of Sacred Scripture, such as God's justice, and apply it to other known truths of Sacred Scripture, such as reward (see Mt 20:23) and punishment in fitting degrees according to what one did in this life (see Rom 2:6). Similar levels of fitting reward and punishment are seen in Dante's treatment of heaven and purgatory.

Sober but Serene on Themes of Judgment in the African-American Spirituals

I've often been impressed at the ability of the old African-American spirituals to treat serious subjects in a clear, memorable, and almost joyful way. This is true even of very weighty matters like sin and judgment. We do well to look at some of the creative lines from different spirituals that articulate this theme.

It can be very helpful to the preacher, teacher, and parent to help recover an ethos of coming judgment but in a way that is almost playfully bright, while at the same time deeply soulful.

In a certain sense, the spirituals are unimpeachable even by hypersensitive post-moderns who seek to shame the preacher for highlighting the sterner biblical themes. Most of the spirituals were written by slaves, who creatively worked biblical themes into songs that helped accompany their work as well as their worship.

As such, they were written in the cauldron of great suffering. If any people might be excused from thinking that the

Lord would exempt them from judgment day, it is surely the enslaved in the deep South. If any people might be excused from crying out for vengeance, it is those enslaved in the South. And yet the spirituals are almost wholly devoid of condemning language; enslaved blacks sang about their own sins and need to be prepared. If they were prepared, God, who knew their trouble, would help them to steal away to Jesus. They did not see themselves as exempt from the need to be ready.

If they, who worked hard in the cotton fields and endured the horrors of slavery, thought these texts applied to them, how much more do they apply to us, who recline on our couches and speak of our freedom to do as we please? So let's sample some of these lines from numerous spirituals that speak to judgment and the last things:

1. *I would not be a sinner, I'll tell you the reason why. I'm afraid my Lord might call my name and I wouldn't be ready to die.*

2. *Some go to Church for to sing and shout, before six months they's all turned out!*

3. *Everybody talkin' 'bout heaven aint a goin' there, Oh my Lord!*

4. *Where shall I be when the first Trumpet sounds, oh where shall I be when it sounds so loud, when it sounds so loud as to wake up the dead, Oh where shall be when it sounds. How will it be with my poor soul, Oh Where Shall I be?*

5. *Better watch my brother how you walk on the cross! Your foot might slip and your soul get lost!*

*6. God gave Noah the rainbow sign, no more water but the fire
next time!*

*7. Old Satan wears a hypocrite's shoe, If you don't watch he'll
slip it on you!*

*8. Noah, Noah let me come in!
The Doors are fastened and the windows pinned!
Noah said, "Ya done lost your track
Can't plow straight! you keep a-lookin' back!"*

*9. Knock at the window; knock at the door
Callin' brother Noah
Can't you take more?!
No said Noah cause you're full of sin!
God has the key you can't get in!*

*10. Well I went to the rock to hide my face
The rock cried out, no hiding place
There's no hiding place down here
Oh the Rock cried I'm burnin' too!
I wanna go to heaven just as much as you!*

*11. Oh sinner man better repent!
for God's gonna call you to judgment.
There's No hiding place down there!*

*12. No signal for another train
To follow in this line
Oh sinner you're forever lost
When once you're left behind.
She's nearing now the station*

Oh, sinner don't be vain
But come and get your ticket
Be ready for that train!

13. *Sinner please don't let this harvest Pass*
And die and lose your soul at last.

14. *My Lord, what a morning, When the stars begin to fall*
You'll hear the trumpet sound, to wake the nations under-
ground
Looking to my God's right hand,
When the stars begin to fall
You'll hear the sinner moan, When the stars begin to fall
You'll hear the Christian shout,
Oh, When the stars begin to fall!

Most of these songs are deeply scriptural and make serious appeals to the human soul, but they do so in a way that is creative. They get you tapping your foot and invite you to a joyful consideration of the need to repent before it's too late. Others are more soulful, even mournful, in their pentatonic scale.

Given all the reticence to discuss the four last things (death, judgment, heaven, and hell), songs like these may help to reopen the door to necessary conversations between preacher and congregation, parents and children. They are a valuable resource.

We can conclude with a creative spiritual about the last judgment. Note that it is rich in biblical references. It is joyful—a real toe-tapper—and makes a serious point along with a wish: "In That Great Gettin' Up Mornin' Fare You Well!" Here's the text (with phonetic spelling):

I'm Gonna tell ya 'bout da comin' of da judgment
Der's a better day a comin',
Fare thee well, fare thee well!

Chorus:
In dat great gettin' up mornin',
Fare thee well, fare thee well
In dat great gettin' up mornin',
Fare thee well, fare thee well

Oh preacher fold yo' bible,
For dat last souls converted,
Fare thee well, fare thee well

Blow yo' trumpet Gabriel,
Lord, how loud shall I blow it?
Blow it right and calm and easy,

Do not alarm all my people,
Tell dem all come to da judgment,
Fare thee well, fare thee well!

Do you see dem coffins burstin,
do you see dem folks is risin'
Do you see dat fork of lightenin',
Do you hear dat rumblin' thunder?!?
Fare thee well, fare thee well!

Do you see dem stars a fallin',
Do you see da world on fire?!?
Fare thee well, fare thee well

Do you see dem Saints is risin',
Fare thee well, fare thee well
See 'em marchin' home for heaven,
Fare thee well, fare thee well

Oh! Fare thee well poor sinner, fare thee well, fare thee well
Fare thee well poor sinner, fare thee well, fare thee well!